10-99

PROGRA[...]
087[8]21
KU-537-440

MADE S[IMP]LE

AT ONLY £10.99 • 200 PAGES • PAPERBACK

77541

If you're a student or home
enthusiast, taking your first steps
in programmin[...]
experienced p[...]
wants to quick[...]
essentials of a[...]
then the Made[...]
programming [...]

[...]h, with tasks to do and easy steps,
Books from Butterworth-Heinemann

• Easy to Follo[w]
• Jargon Free
• Task Based
• Practical Exercises

Thousands of people have already discovered that
the MADE SIMPLE series gives them what they
want fast! Many delighted readers have written,
telephoned and e-mailed us about the Made
Simple Series of computer books. Comments have
included:

• 'Clear, concise and well laid out.'
• 'Ideal for the first time user.'
• 'Clear, accurate, well presented, jargon free,
  well targeted.'
• 'Easy to follow to perform a task.'

[...]

[...]orth recommending

NEW	[Jav]a [P]. McBride [5]06 3241 0	1997
NEW	Java Script P. K. McBride 0 7506 3797 8	1997
NEW	[P]ascal [P.] K. McBride [0] 7506 3242 9	1997
NEW	[C]++ Programming [C]onor Sexton [0] 7506 3243 7	1997
NEW	C Programming Conor Sexton 0 7506 3244 5	1997
NEW	Visual Basic Stephen Morris 0 7506 3245 3	1997
NEW	Delphi Stephen Morris 0 7506 3246 1	1997
NEW	Visual C++ Stephen Morris 0 7506 3570 3	1997
NEW	Unix P. K. McBride 0 7506 3571 1	1997
NEW	Windows 95 Programming Stephen Morris 0 7506 3572 X	1997
NEW	Cobol Programming (for the year 2000) Conor Sexton 0 7506 3834 6	1997

COMPUTING MADE SIMPLE

AT ONLY £8.99 · 160 PAGES · PAPERBACK

BESTSELLER
Works for Windows 3.1 (Version 3)
P. K. McBride
0 7506 2065 X   1994

Lotus 1-2-3 (2.4 DOS Version)
Ian Robertson
0 7506 2066 8   1994

WordPerfect (DOS 6.0)
Stephen Copestake
0 7506 2068 4   1994

BESTSELLER
MS DOS (Up To Version 6.22)
Ian Sinclair
0 7506 2069 2   1994

BESTSELLER
Excel For Windows 3.1 (Version 5)
Stephen Morris
0 7506 2070 6   1994

BESTSELLER
Word For Windows 3.1 (Version 6)
Keith Brindley
0 7506 2071 4   1994

BESTSELLER
Windows 3.1
P. K. McBride
0 7506 2072 2   1994

BESTSELLER
Windows 95
P. K. McBride
0 7506 2306 3   1995

Lotus 1-2-3 for Windows 3.1 (Version 5)
Stephen Morris
0 7506 2307 1   1995

BESTSELLER
Access For Windows 3.1 (Version 2)
Moira Stephen
0 7506 2309 8   1995

BESTSELLER
Internet for Windows 3.1
P. K. McBride
0 7506 2311 X   1995

Pageplus for Windows 3.1 (Version 3)
Ian Sinclair
0 7506 2312 8   1995

Hard Drives
Ian Sinclair
0 7506 2313 6   1995

BESTSELLER
Multimedia for Windows 3.1
Simon Collin
0 7506 2314 4   1995

Powerpoint for Windows 3.1 (Version 4.0)
Moira Stephen
0 7506 2420 5   1995

Office 95
P. K. McBride
0 7506 2625 9   1995

Word Pro for Windows 3.1 (Version 4.0)
Moira Stephen
0 7506 2626 7   1995

BESTSELLER
Word for Windows 95 (Version 7)
Keith Brindley
0 7506 2815 4   1996

BESTSELLER
Excel for Windows 95 (Version 7)
Stephen Morris
0 7506 2816 2   1996

Powerpoint for Windows 95 (Version 7)
Moira Stephen
0 7506 2817 0   1996

BESTSELLER
Access for Windows 95 (Version 7)
Moira Stephen
0 7506 2818 9   1996

BESTSELLER
Internet for Windows 95
P. K. McBride
0 7506 2835 9   1996

Internet Resources
P. K. McBride
0 7506 2836 7   1996

Microsoft Networking
P. K. McBride
0 7506 2837 5   1996

Designing Internet Home Pages
Lilian Hobbs
0 7506 2941 X   1996

BESTSELLER
Works for Windows 95 (Version 4.0)
P. K. McBride
0 7506 3396 4   1996

NEW
Windows NT (Version 4.0)
Lilian Hobbs
0 7506 3511 8   1997

NEW
Compuserve
Keith Brindley
0 7506 3512 6   1997

NEW
Microsoft Internet Explorer
Sam Kennington
0 7506 3513 4   1997

NEW
Netscape Navigator
Sam Kennington
0 7506 3514 2   1997

NEW
Searching The Internet
Sam Kennington
0 7506 3794 3   1997

NEW
The Internet for Windows 3.1 (Second Edition)
P. K. McBride
0 7506 3795 1   1997

NEW
The Internet for Windows 95 (Second Edition)
P. K. McBride
0 7506 3846 X   1997

NEW
Office 97 for Windows
P. K. McBride
0 7506 3798 6   1997

NEW
Powerpoint 97 For Windows
Moira Stephen
0 7506 3799 4   1997

NEW
Access 97 For Windows
Moira Stephen
0 7506 3800 1   1997

NEW
Word 97 For Windows
Keith Brindley
0 7506 3801 X   1997

NEW
Excel 97 For Windows
Stephen Morris
0 7506 3802 8   1997

Visual C++
Made Simple

Stephen Morris

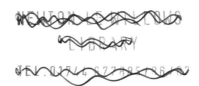

Made Simple
BOOKS

Made Simple
An imprint of Butterworth-Heinemann
Linacre House, Jordan Hill, Oxford OX2 8DP
A division of Reed Educational and Professional Publishing Ltd

Ⓡ A member of the Reed Elsevier plc group

OXFORD   BOSTON   JOHANNESBURG

MELBOURNE   NEW DELHI   SINGAPORE

First published 1998

© Stephen Morris 1998

TRADEMARKS/REGISTERED TRADEMARKS
Computer hardware and software brand names mentioned in this book are protected
by their respective trademarks and are acknowledged.

British Library Cataloguing in Publication Data
A catalogue record for this book is available from the British Library

ISBN 0 7506 3570 3

Typeset by Butford Technical Publishing, Bodenham, Hereford
Archetype, Bash Casual, Cotswold and Gravity fonts from Advanced Graphics Ltd
Icons designed by Sarah Ward © 1994

Printed and bound in Great Britain by Scotprint Ltd, Musselburgh, Scotland.

Contents

Preface

Visual C++ provides an efficient programming system for writing Windows applications. The language has the capability to generate the complete range of software, from simple dialog-based programs to multi-user applications and operating systems.

Visual C++ incorporates a number of separate tools, amongst which is the Developer Studio, a sophisticated environment for the production of Windows user interfaces and the development of code.

The language around which Visual C++ is based relies heavily on the principles of object-oriented programming and, as such, is not a tool for newcomers to programming. However, its complexity, though intimidating for the first-time user, does provide methods that can be used to solve almost any computer problem. The latest versions of Visual C++ have been designed specifically for the 32-bit environments of Windows 95 and Windows NT.

The lack of any detailed user guides makes initial use of C++ an awesome undertaking; finding out how to do even the simplest of tasks from the on-line help alone is a daunting task and, although the documentation is extensive, there is little introductory material available. The aim of this book is to fill part of that gap.

The book is intended for those who are new to Visual C++ but some familiarity with the C and C++ languages is assumed. This book concentrates on the 'visual' aspects of the environment. Those who need an introduction to C or C++ should refer to *C Programming Made Simple* and *C++ Programming Made Simple*. Both books provide an excellent starting point for developing C programming skills.

Visual C++ is comprehensive and complex, and a book of this size can only give a brief introduction. However, the information given here should be enough to give you a flavour of Visual C++ and show you its potential for developing professional Windows applications.

Acknowledgements

I would like to thank Microsoft Corporation for their assistance while this book was in preparation.

1 Overview

Starting Visual C++

Visual C++ provides a comprehensive 32-bit programming environment, in which many different types of application can be created. The powerful Developer Studio component of the environment lets you design the user interface for an application quickly and easily; it also generates all the code needed to run your application in a 32-bit Windows system. This code, written in the C++ programming language, can then be extended to create an application that responds to the user's actions. Visual C++ is not easy to master but it does provide access to every aspect of Windows programming.

Visual C++ editions

The latest version of Visual C++ comes in three editions:

- *Learning Edition* – creates fully-functional Windows applications using a set of standard tools

- *Professional Edition* – adds the tools necessary to create distributable applications for all 32-bit PC environments

- *Enterprise Edition* – includes facilities for setting up client/server applications

This book concentrates on those features of the Professional Edition that are common to all three editions.

Take note

Although the Learning Edition contains everything you need for creating self-contained Window applications you may not distribute your finished applications to other users.

Windows versions

Visual C++ is supplied only as a 32-bit version and must therefore be run under Windows 95, Windows NT 4.0 or later versions of Windows. Applications created with Visual C++ can be run only under 32-bit versions of Windows.

Installation

Visual C++ is installed in a similar way to most other Windows applications.

1   Load the Visual C++ CD. Select Setup.exe from the CD's root directory.

2   Click on Install Visual C++ and follow the instructions as they appear on screen.

At the end of the set-up process, the installation program will add an option to the Programs menu, leading to the main Visual C++ program plus some subsidiary programs.

Tip

If you are short of hard disk space you do not have to install the whole application (which requires about 280Mb); instead, select the Custom installation and choose only the features you need. For instance, you may omit the database tools or the on-line 'books'. The missing parts can be added later by re-running the installation program.

Visual C++ folder

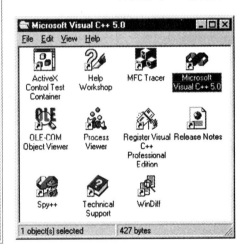

Tip

For easy access, you can create a Visual C++ folder and shortcut icon. In Explorer, open the Windows | Start Menu | Programs folder and copy the Microsoft Visual C++ folder icon to the Windows | Desktop folder (click on the C++ folder, hold down [Ctrl] and drag the folder onto 'Desktop').

Running Visual C++

The installation process will have created a number of menu options and icons, which will run the application and access other C++ tools.

Starting the program

1 Minimise any other applications that are currently running and minimise any folders.

2 Click on the Start button, then on Programs, the Microsoft Visual C++ folder icon and, finally, on the Visual C++ program icon.

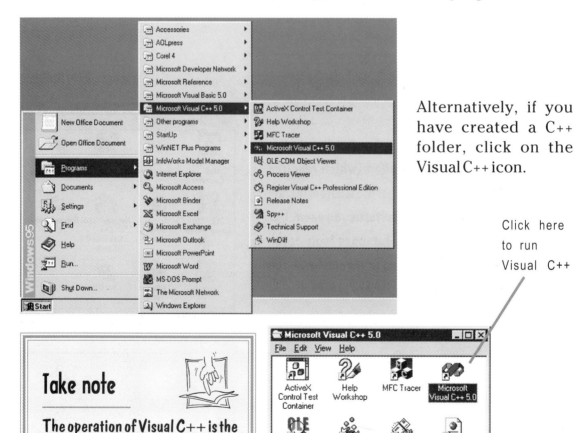

Alternatively, if you have created a C++ folder, click on the Visual C++ icon.

Click here to run Visual C++

Take note

The operation of Visual C++ is the same in all 32-bit versions of Windows. In this book, the illustrations are taken from Windows 95.

The Visual C++ display

The first time you load Visual C++, you will be presented with a rather confusing collection of menus, toolbars and windows. This display will change as you begin to develop applications and you can also modify it to suit the way you work. The next time you load Visual C++ the display will be as you left it.

Project Workspace window ('docked'), lists available on-line help topics

Main window – select actions from menus or toolbar

Main entry point for on-line help

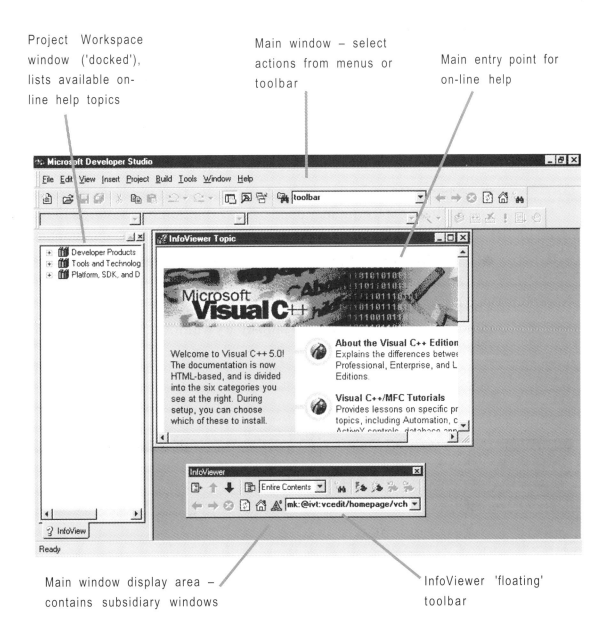

Main window display area – contains subsidiary windows

InfoViewer 'floating' toolbar

Visual C++ windows

The Visual C++ display consists of a main window and a number of subsidiary windows. It is well worth familiarising yourself with the most important windows before you start creating an application.

Main window

The **main window** contains all the elements you would expect to find in a Windows application:

- The **title bar** will show the name of your current project and include the usual buttons for minimising, maximising and closing the window.

- The **menu bar** includes nine drop-down menus. Many of the options in these menus are described later in the book.

- The **toolbars** contain a number of icons that provide shortcuts to the most frequently used operations, such as saving a file or loading help topics.

- The **status bar**, at the bottom of the window, displays messages and other system information.

The main part of the window, between the toolbars and status bar, may contain a number of other subsidiary windows. This is where you develop your applications.

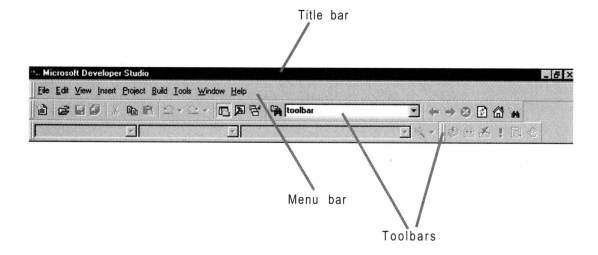

Title bar

Menu bar

Toolbars

Subsidiary windows

The first time you load Visual C++, the main window contains the **Project Workspace** window on the left. You can expand this window to fill all the available space in the main window by clicking on the maximise button.

Minimise within main window
Expand to fill main window
Close subsidiary window

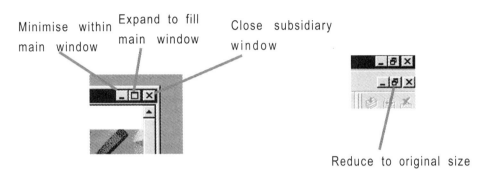

Reduce to original size

You can also minimise or close the subsidiary window, or reduce it to its original size.

Floating and docked windows

The position of the toolbars and other windows can also be changed. A floating window (such as the InfoViewer toolbar) can be docked by dragging its title bar to any edge of the main window; the docked window changes shape to fit along the edge.

Drag to change position or 'dock' window

Click to close window

Any docked window, can be turned into a floating window (including all the toolbars and the Project Workspace window) by dragging any unused part of the window into the middle of the screen.

Drag to move or 'float'

7

The latest version of Visual C++ is supplied with virtually no printed documentation. Therefore, if you need help with any aspect of the system you must use the on-line help. This comes as a series of 'books', presented as a tree structure in the Project Workspace window. This tree forms a contents list for the help topics. Each book contains a number of chapters, each of which contains one or more help topics. Double-clicking on the icons in the tree opens and closes items.

The on-line help is provided as HTML documents, giving it the same look as an Internet site. The standard web-browser methods are available for moving from page to page, or you can select pages from the InfoView tree. The InfoViewer toolbar provides icons to help you move around the text. Even so, tracking down the solution to a problem can be time-consuming and you may need to piece together several help topics in order to get a meaningful answer to your question.

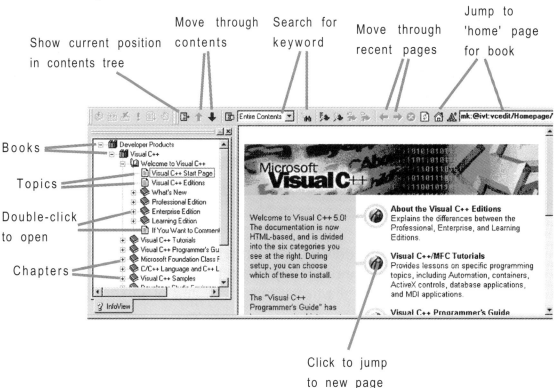

Help options

You can get on-line help in a number of other ways:

● Click on Help in the menu bar at the top of the main window and then on Contents in the drop-down menu. This re-opens the Project Workspace window if it has been closed.

● Click on the Search icon on the InfoViewer toolbar to display the Index list (or select Keyword Search from the Help menu). The main part of this window lists the topics available in on-line help; you can either scroll through the list or start typing in the text box at the top to go straight to an item in the index. Double-click on an index item; this will either show the corresponding help or list relevant topics.

● Press function key **[F1]** (context-sensitive help) to go straight to the topic relating to your current activity. For instance, if you click on the Project Workspace window and press **[F1]** you will get (very limited) information on InfoView. You can also get context-sensitive help on specific parts of a dialog box, error messages and individual keywords when writing code.

When you select help for the first time you are given the opportunity to connect to the Internet; click on Cancel.

When you have finished with the help screen, remove it by clicking on the close button.

Type text to find index entry

Double-click on an item to show related topics

Double-click on a topic to display help screen

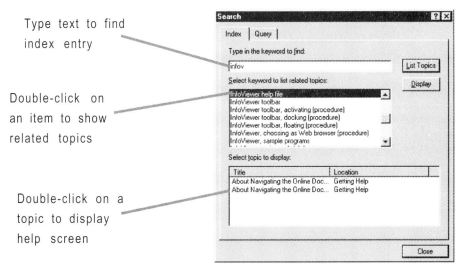

Exercises

1   Start Visual C++ and identify the windows that are displayed.

2   Close individual windows and then re-open them again. Move the windows to more convenient positions; resize them where appropriate. Minimise the help window and main window, then restore them.

3   Search for help relating to the use of InfoViewer to access the internet.

For solutions to these exercises, see page 174.

2 Applications

Creating an application

The work of creating an application is done using a part of the Visual C++ environment called the **Developer Studio**. The Developer Studio includes a 'wizard' – a series of dialog boxes that guide you through a process – to help you create an application from scratch. Even the simplest C++ application, which does nothing but display a single window, comprises several files and many lines of complex code. However, this essential code is similar for all applications and will be generated for you.

1 Select New from the File menu; the New dialog box is displayed. If necessary, click on the Projects tab.

Click Projects tab

Type project name

Select directory

Choose application type

Click on OK when ready

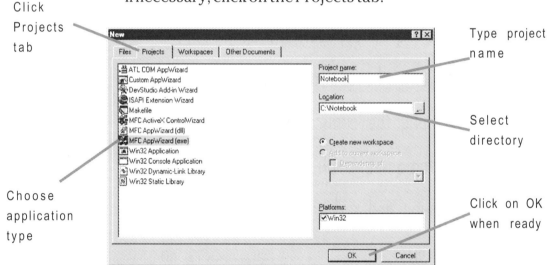

2 Select the relevant wizard for the type of application you wish to create. To start with, this will be the **MFC AppWizard (exe)** option, which creates executable files based on the Microsoft Foundation Classes (described later).

Take note

When you are an experienced Visual C++ developer, you will use the other options to develop other types of applications.

3 Give the project a suitable name.

4 In the Location box, select the directory where the development files are to be stored (this directory will be created if it does not exist).

5 Since this is your first project, accept the option to create a new **workspace**. The **platform** is Win32, indicating that the application will be run in Windows 32-bit environments.

Take note

A project is a collection of files and configuration information needed to build an application. The workspace is the area that holds these files.

The MFC AppWizard

The MFC AppWizard allows you to create three different types of application:

- **Dialog-based** applications, which have a dialog box as their front-end user interface (e.g. Calculator, Character Map and ScanDisk).

- **Single Document Interface** (SDI) applications, which consist of a frame (containing menu, toolbars and status bar) around a data area (e.g. Notepad and Paint).

- **Multiple Document Interface** (MDI) applications, which have a main frame that contains one or more child windows (e.g. Microsoft Word and Excel).

Before you start, you need to decide which sort of application you are creating.

AppWizard steps

The wizard leads you through a number of dialog boxes before creating the application for you. In most cases you can accept the default options.

Step 1   Select the application type. The first example in this chapter uses an MDI application. At the end of the chapter, a dialog-based application is created.

Step 2   Choose the type of database support you require (**None** unless you need to link the application to an existing database).

Step 3   Specify the way in which you want to link to other applications (**None**, unless you want to embed objects from other applications). Accept the option to support ActiveX controls.

Step 4   Choose the features to be included in the application. Most of the defaults should be satisfactory but you will probably want to add context-sensitive help. In the Advanced dialog you might want to enter a default extension and corresponding description for data files created by your application.

Tip

Click on the Context-sensitive Help button if you think there is any likelihood that you may want to provide detailed user help for your application.

Visual C++ will add appropriate 'hooks' in your programs, which you can ignore if you decide not to supply help; adding in these hooks manually later is time-consuming and prone to errors.

Click to
add help

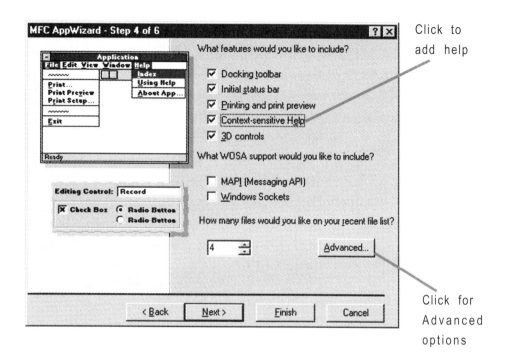

Click for
Advanced
options

Advanced options

Enter
extension

Change if
necessary

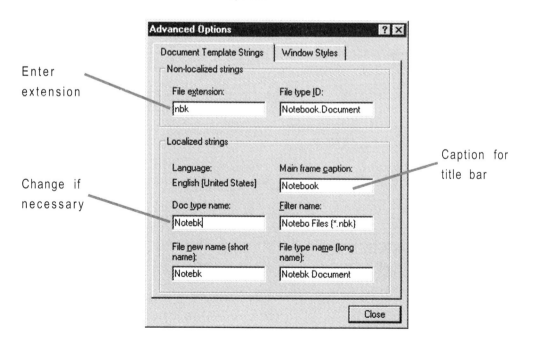

Caption for
title bar

Step 5   Accept the options to generate source file comments and to use the MFC library as a shared DLL.

If you use the shared DLL, you will have to supply the standard DLL to your users but the application itself will be much smaller. (Many users will already have the DLL for use with other MFC applications.) If you statically link the library, the MFC procedures you have used are included in the EXE file itself, making it much larger.

Step 6   The wizard lists the classes it is going to create. Clicking on any of these shows at the bottom of the box the names of the files it will create. Although you can change these, there is little point in doing so.

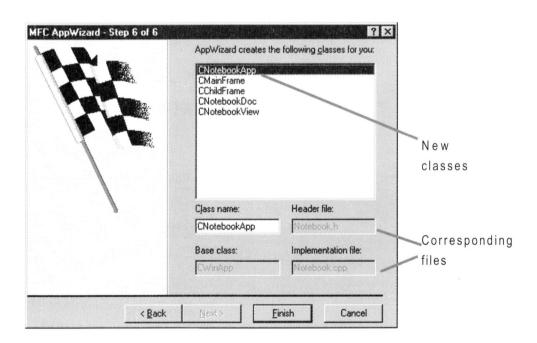

When you click on Finish, the wizard displays a detailed description of the application that is about to be created. Click on OK to start the process.

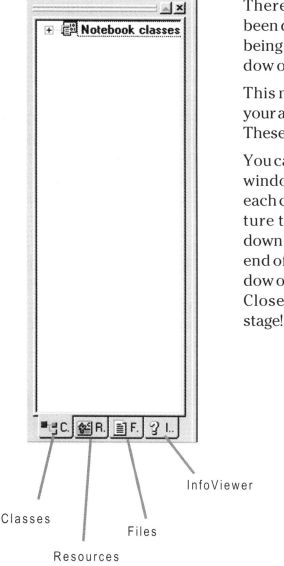

Classes

Resources

Files

InfoViewer

There is little to show for the work that has been done by the wizard, the only visible sign being a change in the Project Workspace window on the left of the screen.

This now has three new tabs, for displaying your application's classes, resources and files. These are discussed in detail in later chapters.

You can view the different components of this window by clicking on any of the four tabs. In each case, you are presented with a tree structure that can be opened up or closed back down again. Double-clicking on any item at the end of the tree's branches will open up a window of some sort; to close it again, click on the Close button. Don't change anything at this stage!

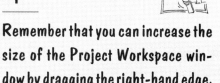

Tip

Remember that you can increase the size of the Project Workspace window by dragging the right-hand edge, if necessary.

Take note

The main entry for the Classes tab is shown as 'Notebook classes' for this example; the name is based on the application name.

Building the application

As you will see later, the project is made up of many different C++ files. Visual C++ needs to go through several stages in order to **build** these files into the final application.

The first stage is to compile the individual program files into code that the computer can understand. The compiler starts by invoking the **preprocessor**, which performs preliminary tasks such as including files of code that have been created separately and checking for compilation conditions. For example, you may specify that a certain section of code should be included only under a certain condition; if this condition is not met, the code will be excluded by the preprocessor,

When the preprocessor has finished its work, the compiler translates the file of C++ code into an **object file**. This file contains machine code and further compilation instructions. For instance, there will be references to functions in external libraries. At this point, the compiler knows nothing about those functions, apart from their names. Therefore the machine code in the object file is incomplete and cannot be run as a program.

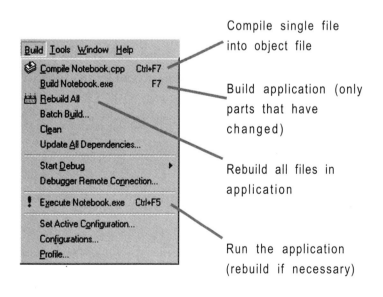

Compile single file into object file

Build application (only parts that have changed)

Rebuild all files in application

Run the application (rebuild if necessary)

The final stage is to **link** the compiled files together, creating an executable application file. The linker matches functions references in the compiled files to actual functions in the libraries; in this way, it fills in any gaps in the machine code and produces code that should run successfully.

The Developer Studio Build menu provides options for performing individual parts of the build process or carrying out the entire process at once. By far the laziest (and usually most appropriate) method is to use the Execute option. This option compiles any C++ files that have changed since the last build, links the files to create a new executable file and then (if no errors are encountered) runs the application.

When you build an application, a new window appears at the bottom of the Developer Studio main window, showing the progress of the build process. The first time you build an application there should be no problems but later, as you add your own code, any errors will be listed here as well.

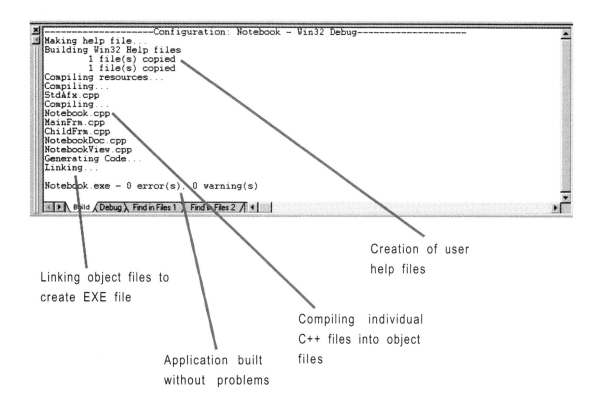

Linking object files to create EXE file

Creation of user help files

Compiling individual C++ files into object files

Application built without problems

To see more of this window, drag its top border upwards.

Running the application

The application you have created can now be run. It doesn't do very much, though you might be surprised by the amount of functionality it does contain, given that you have not yet had to write a line of code.

Click on the Build I Execute menu option or press **[Ctrl-F5]**. If you have not yet built the application, you are asked for confirmation that the EXE file is to be created. The application will be compiled and linked (if necessary), then run. To start with, it consists of a main window and one child window.

Title of application and title
of current child window (as
defined in Step 4, Advanced)

Main
window

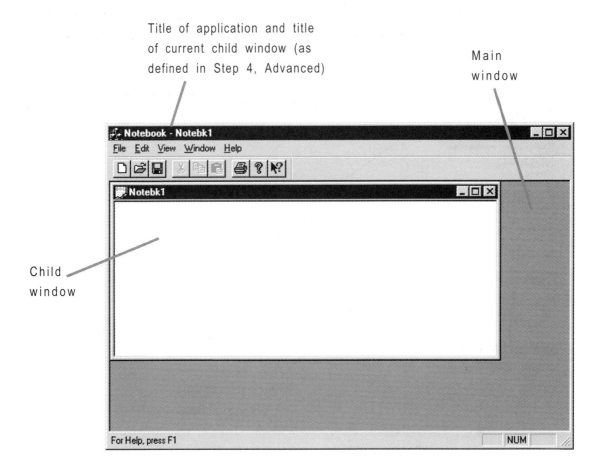

Child
window

You new application embodies all the functionality you would expect to find in a standard Windows application – with virtually no effort on your part.

● The main window can be dragged to a new position, resized, minimised, maximised and closed.

● There are a set of menus, a toolbar and a status bar.

● The File menu contains all the standard Windows options, with corresponding buttons on the toolbar for New, Open, Save and Print.

● The File | New option creates another child window, giving it a default name. File | Close closes the current child window.

● The Open, Save and Save As options bring up standard Open | Save dialog boxes, listing files with the extension you specified when creating the application. You can also list all files.

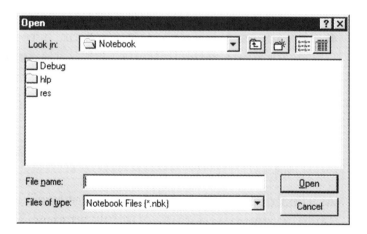

● The File menu lists the four most recently opened files.

● The Print, Print Preview and Print Setup options are fully functional (though there is no data there to print yet).

● The Edit menu has a full set of options, with corresponding toolbar buttons (all currently greyed out, as there is not yet any data to edit).

- The View menu switches on and off the display of the toolbar and status bar.

- The Window menu lists the open child windows and lets you re-arrange them.

- The Help menu leads you to a working help program, with help already there for the functions built into your application.

- Help | About displays the name of your program with a copyright notice (showing the current year). There is also an About button on the toolbar.

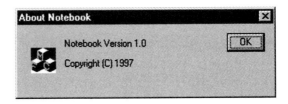

- If you rest the pointer on a button, a 'tool tip' pops up and a description of the button's function is displayed on the status bar.

- The last button on the toolbar – Help – loads the Help program for any feature you click on.

- The child windows can be moved and resized within the main window.

As a final demonstration of the power of AppWizard, use File | Save to save the (empty) contents of a child window. Then close down your program (File | Exit) and run Explorer. In the application directory you will find a Document file, of size 0kB, with the filename you gave it and your default extension. Double-click on this file and Windows will run your new application! If you look at the File Types tab in Explorer's View | Options menu item you will see that your default extension has been added to the list of registered file types.

Dialog-based applications

Dialog-based applications are even simpler to create than MDI or SDI applications. The same MFC AppWizard is used but it has fewer steps and fewer choices.

If you still have your MDI application open, close it down with the File | Close Workspace option. Using File | New, give the project a suitable name and run the MFC AppWizard.

Step 1   Select the application type – Dialog based.

Step 2   Choose the features to be included. Add context-sensitive help if you think you may want to include help later.

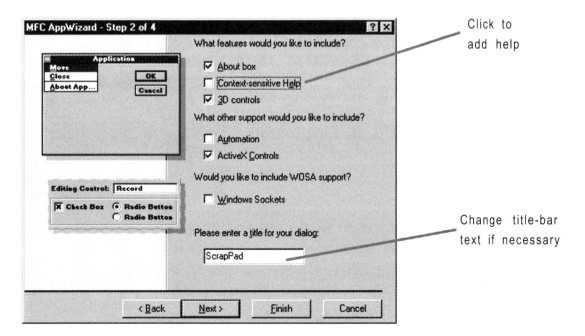

Click to add help

Change title-bar text if necessary

Step 3   Accept the options to generate source file comments and to use the shared DLL.

Step 4   The wizard lists the new classes; this time there are only two (see next page). Click on Finish.

The AppWizard displays a description of the application, then generates the application's files.

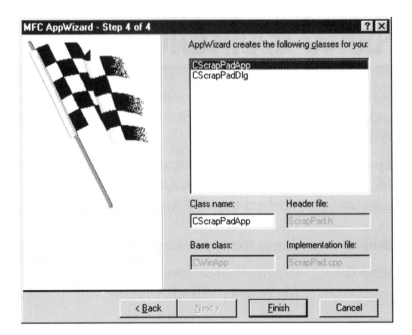

Building and running the application

The options in the Build menu are the same as for MDI applications. Choosing the Execute option builds the EXE file and then runs it.

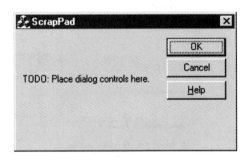

The dialog box is very simple, though it contains all the usual Windows functionality.

● The box can be moved by dragging the title bar.

● There are either two or three buttons: standard OK and Cancel buttons and (if the Context-sensitive Help box was clicked) a Help button.

● Clicking on OK or Cancel, clicking on the Close button, or pressing the **[Esc]** key all close down the application.

● Clicking on the Help button runs an almost-empty Help program.

Finally, in case you needed the reminder, there is a label telling you that you need to add other controls (buttons and other objects).

When you have finished with the application, select File I Close Workspace.

Leaving and restarting Visual C++

Visual C++ has all the usual Windows options for suspending it or for closing it down, and restarting C++ with your previous application is very straightforward.

Leaving Visual C++

You can suspend Visual C++ temporarily by minimising the main window or simply selecting another active application. To get back into C++, click on its taskbar button, click on any visible part of the C++ window or press **[Alt-Esc]** or **[Alt-Tab]** until Visual C++ is active.

To close Visual C++ down completely, select File | Exit or click on the main window's close button. If you have changed any of the files that make up your application you will be given the opportunity to save them.

Restarting Visual C++

When you next run Visual C++, the main window will be as you left it but with no files loaded. To continue working with your application select File | Recent Workspaces. Your application should be at the top of the pop-up list.

Workspaces are described in the next chapter.

Take note

If you close any of the subsidiary windows within the main window, there is no effect on the application files and Visual C++ continues running. Only by closing the main window will you exit Visual C++, closing all subsidiary windows at the same time.

Take note

When you build the application, all the files are saved. If you don't perform a build for some time you should regularly save all files.

Exercises

1 Create an MDI application called VisDraw. (This application will allow you to draw or write text on a window.)

2 Build and run the application and check that everything works.

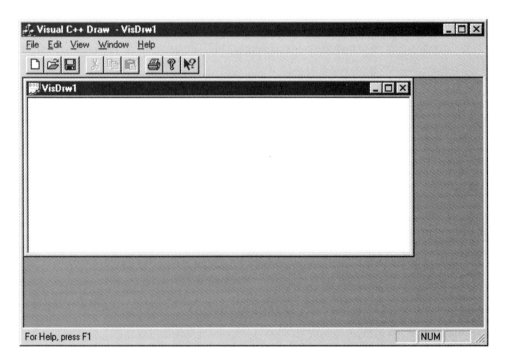

3 Create a dialog-based application called VisCalc. (This application will provide calculator functions.)

4 Build and run the application, then close it down.

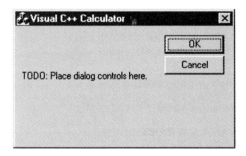

For solutions to these exercises, see page 174.

3 Exploring the application

Object-oriented programming (OOP)

In less time than it takes to boil a kettle, the AppWizard has built for you a fully functioning Windows application – something that would take you many weeks to accomplish if you had to do it from scratch. So you can afford to spend a few minutes, while you drink a cup of tea, familiarising yourself with the file AppWizard has created on your behalf.

There are many new files, all filled with sections of seemingly incomprehensible code. Some of this code is explained later in this book, as it is modified and expanded; some you will learn about as you become more experienced and expand the capabilities of your applications; and some you will never need to touch, so it may be ignored. Most importantly, you need an understanding of the object-oriented structure of your application and the OOP jargon you are likely to encounter.

Objects and their use

In traditional programming systems, a program consists of a linear series of instructions, through which control flows in an ordered and predictable manner; data is stored separately from the program. Object-oriented programs, on the other hand, have a much looser structure, in which programs and data are bound together in independent units and control lies firmly in the hands of the user.

The windows in your application and their components – command buttons, labels, scroll bars, menus etc. – are all **objects**. An object is self-contained; it comprises both the procedures to perform its required tasks and the data that these procedures need. In a process called **encapsulation**, the procedures and data are insulated from the rest of the program. There should be no danger of control jumping unexpectedly from one object's procedures into the middle of those of another object; nor should it be possible for one object to inadvertently change the data belonging to another object.

Information – data and instructions – is passed between objects in the form of **messages**. For instance, when a button is clicked, Windows sends a particular message to the button object. The button-click procedure is executed and another message is sent back to say that the action has been processed.

All objects of the same type come from the same **class**. The class defines the procedures and data for the object. Visual C++ uses a set of related classes called the **Microsoft Foundation Classes** (MFC) and all objects in your programs will be derived from one of these classes. For instance, all command buttons come from a class called CButton. (All MFC classes begin with 'C'.) The class is a template for objects of that type; individual objects are created as **instances** of that class.

The appearance of an object – and to a certain extent its behaviour – is determined by its **properties**: specific data values encapsulated within the object. For example, two windows from the same class may have different text in the title bar; whether or not they can be minimised is determined by the value of another property.

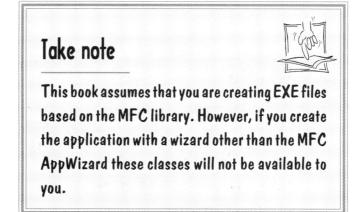

Take note

This book assumes that you are creating EXE files based on the MFC library. However, if you create the application with a wizard other than the MFC AppWizard these classes will not be available to you.

When a class has been defined, a new class can be derived from it. Initially, the new class will have all the procedures and data from the original class (the **base** class); this is called **inheritance**. Some of the data structures and procedures are changed in the new class, giving its objects different behaviour and appearance to those of the original class.

For example, CButton is derived from a general class of controls called CWnd; CButton has all the features of CWnd but modifies and extends them to produce a variety of buttons.

Similarly, CBitmapButton is derived from CButton and results in buttons that have pictures instead of text on their surface.

CEdit and CStatic are also derived from CWnd but modify the class in slightly different ways to produce edit boxes and labels respectively. Therefore, CButton, CEdit and CStatic share many characteristics but have their own unique features; this is known as **polymorphism**.

Take note

The values of the properties for CButton determine whether the object is a command button, radio button or check box.

Take note

Technically, buttons, combo boxes, labels and other controls are all 'windows' (as are normal windows and dialog boxes), since they are all derived from CWnd.

Most classes in the MFC library are derived from a single class, CObject, and together they form the **class hierarchy**. A small part of this hierarchy is illustrated below.

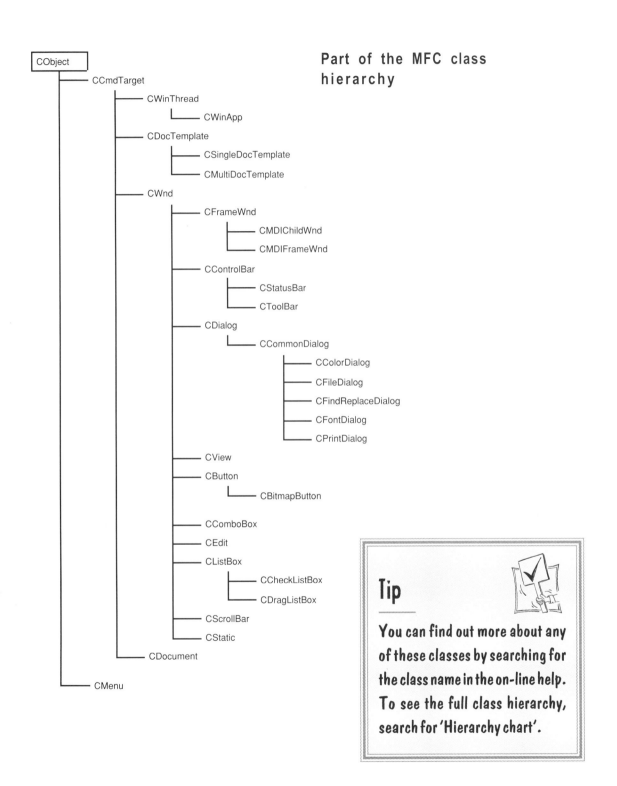

Part of the MFC class hierarchy

Tip

You can find out more about any of these classes by searching for the class name in the on-line help. To see the full class hierarchy, search for 'Hierarchy chart'.

The ClassView

The AppWizard has generated a number of classes for you. The names of these classes will vary, depending on the name of the application. The classes will also depend on whether you have generated a multi-document, single-document or dialog-based application. First, consider the MDI classes.

The new classes can be viewed in the Project Workspace window on the left of the Developer Studio window. The **workspace** is the area that contains your project and all related files.

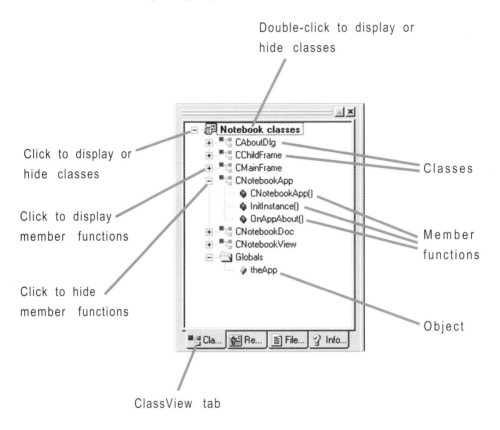

Click the ClassView button if the correct pane is not yet displayed.

Double-clicking on the application classes icon at the top of the window lists the classes. Clicking on the '+' icon to the left of a class name opens up the class to list its member functions; clicking on the icon again closes the list.

Classes

An MDI application contains the following classes (see diagram on page 34):

- **CnameApp**: the main application class, which controls all other classes – derived from CWinApp

- **CnameDoc**: the document class, which handles the data for the application (including loading and saving files) – derived from CDocument

- **CnameView**: the view class, which displays the data and allows the user to interact with the application – derived from CView

- **CChildFrame**: the child window class, which holds the view – derived from CMDIChildWnd

- **CMainFrame**: the main window for the application, containing the child windows – derived from CMDIFrameWnd

- **CAboutDlg**: the 'About' dialog box, accessed via the Help | About menu option – derived from CDialog

These classes are described in more detail later.

Member functions

Each class contains several **member functions**, which are procedures that perform specific tasks. For example, the application class contains three member functions:

- **CnameApp**: the **constructor** for the class, which is called when the object is created.

- **InitInstance**: the initialisation procedure, called following the constructor and used to set up the object prior to use.

- **OnAppAbout**: the procedure that is called when the user selects the Help | About option.

The other classes contain many more member functions, which are explained as they are needed. (Many of these need never be changed, so are not described in this book.)

Objects

When you run the application, objects are created from the classes. For example, each time you open a new child window another object is created, based on CChildFrame.

The application itself has one main object, theApp, based on *Cname*App, the main application class.

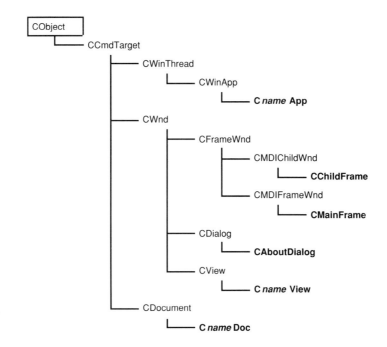

The ResourceView

The second tab on the Project Workspace window displays the new application's resources. A **resource** is an object that is defined in a file separate from the main application file. Resources include objects such as bitmaps, icons, cursors, menus, shortcut keys, toolbars, dialog boxes, text strings and application version information.

Resources are developed independently of applications and combined with them in the final stage of compilation. This independence means that you can change the appearance or behaviour of a resource and then recompile just the resource file, without having to recompile all the other files in the application. The same resource file can be used many times over, giving the same 'look and feel' to all your applications.

Take note

Windows uses resources as part of its memory-management operations. Unless specified otherwise, Windows does not load a resource into memory until needed. Therefore, this part of memory can be used for other purposes when resources are not in use.

The ResourceView contains a number of folders, each of which holds resources of one particular type. Clicking on the '+' icon opens or closes a folder, as does double-clicking on the folder icon.

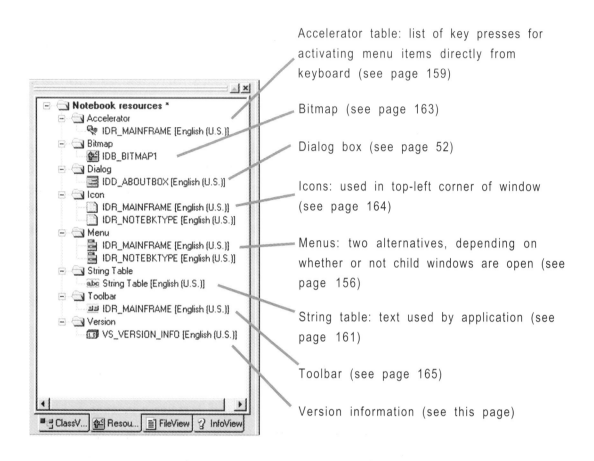

Accelerator table: list of key presses for activating menu items directly from keyboard (see page 159)

Bitmap (see page 163)

Dialog box (see page 52)

Icons: used in top-left corner of window (see page 164)

Menus: two alternatives, depending on whether or not child windows are open (see page 156)

String table: text used by application (see page 161)

Toolbar (see page 165)

Version information (see this page)

Double-clicking on any of the resources loads the appropriate editor for the resource type. The resource can then be edited.

For example, if you double-click on VS_VERSION_INFO you are taken into the Version Information editor. You can enter general information relating to the application here. This information is not used directly by the program (though there is a function for retrieving the data, if it is needed); its main purpose is to annotate the application development. (The version information in the About box is changed by editing the dialog box directly.)

The other resource editors are described later in the book.

The FileView

The ClassView and ResourceView provide a means for inspecting and editing the contents of the various files that make up the project. The FileView lets you list the project files and edit them directly. Click on the third tab in the Project Workspace window to show this view of the project.

In a similar manner to the other two views, the files are grouped into a number of folders, which can be opened and closed by double-clicking.

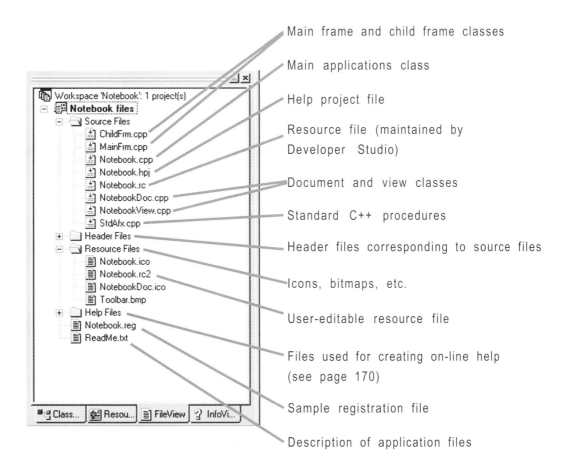

Main frame and child frame classes

Main applications class

Help project file

Resource file (maintained by Developer Studio)

Document and view classes

Standard C++ procedures

Header files corresponding to source files

Icons, bitmaps, etc.

User-editable resource file

Files used for creating on-line help (see page 170)

Sample registration file

Description of application files

The source files are mainly CPP files. These contain the C++ source code and there is one CPP file for each of the main classes. For example, the MainFrm.cpp contains the code for the CMainFrame class (which is derived from the MFC CMDIFrameWnd class). The file named after the application (*name*.cpp) contains the source code for the main application class (C*name*App).

There is a header file, with an H extension, corresponding to each of the CPP source files. The header and source files contain declarations and definitions:

● The header files contains **definitions** of classes; within these definitions are the **declarations** of the new and changed member functions.

● The header file contains **definitions** of the member functions, corresponding to the **declarations** of in the class definition.

Examples of declarations and definitions are given on the following pages.

The Resource Files folder contains the files from the RES subdirectory of your application directory. The contents of these files are accessed from the ResourceView pane; you must not edit the main RC file from outside Visual C++. (You can edit the RC2 file manually, should you need resources that are separate to the main resource file.)

The Help Files folder contains a large number of files used in the compilation of the application's on-line help.

The files you may have to edit are introduced as they are needed.

The main application header file

Before adding to the application, it is worth taking a more detailed look at two of the files: the header and source files for the application itself (e.g. Notebook.h and Notebook.cpp). You don't have to understand everything in these files but it's useful to have an idea of how they are constructed.

Header file contents

The main header file (Notebook.h) contains the declaration of the main application class. Lines starting with two slashes (//) are comments added by Developer Studio.

The first block of code is a sophisticated way of ensuring that the header code is only included once when the application is compiled. The '#if !defined' statement at the beginning may be interpreted as: 'Compile the following statements if the they have not been defined already'. (The ! symbol means 'not' in C++ code.) The end of this conditional block is marked by the corresponding '#endif' statement, right at the end of the header.

The main purpose of the header file is to define the application class. The relevant block of code begins with a **declaration** of the new class:

```
class CNotebookApp : public CWinApp
```

This statement says that you are creating a class called CNotebookApp and that it is to be derived from CWinApp. The **definition** of the class immediately follows, enclosed in braces ({}).

Take note

You don't have to edit this file very often; most of the changes are made for you by the Visual C++ ClassWizard, which is described later.

Tip

To view the header file, either double-click on it in FileView or double-click on the corresponding class in ClassView. After editing, click on the file editor's close button.

Main header file

```
// Notebook.h : main header file for the NOTEBOOK application
//

#if      !defined(AFX_NOTEBOOK_H__C62725B7_...__INCLUDED_)
#define      AFX_NOTEBOOK_H__C62725B7_...__INCLUDED_

#if _MSC_VER >= 1000
#pragma once
#endif // _MSC_VER >= 1000

#ifndef __AFXWIN_H__
    #error include 'stdafx.h' before including this file for PCH
#endif

#include "resource.h"         // main symbols

/////////////////////////////////////////////////////////////////////
// CNotebookApp:
// See Notebook.cpp for the implementation of this class
//

class CNotebookApp : public CWinApp
{
public:
    CNotebookApp();

// Overrides
    // ClassWizard generated virtual function overrides
    //{{AFX_VIRTUAL(CNotebookApp)
    public:
    virtual BOOL InitInstance();
    //}}AFX_VIRTUAL

// Implementation
    //{{AFX_MSG(CNotebookApp)
    afx_msg void OnAppAbout();
        // NOTE - ClassWizard will add/remove member fns here.
        //     DO NOT EDIT these blocks of generated code !
    //}}AFX_MSG
    DECLARE_MESSAGE_MAP()
};

/////////////////////////////////////////////////////////////////////
//{{AFX_INSERT_LOCATION}}
// MS Dev Studio will insert declarations immed. before prev. line.

#endif //
!defined(AFX_NOTEBOOK_H__C62725B7_...__INCLUDED_)
```

Conditional compilation directive (some text omitted)

Include resource header file

Definition of main application class

Class member functions

40

Class member functions

The base class, CWinApp, contains nearly everything your application needs. This functionality is provided by the CWinApp **functions**: procedures for performing specific tasks. CNotebookApp is derived from CWinApp and therefore contains all of the functions from that class (which we will never actually see).

However, we need some functions that are specific to the new application. This is done in one of two ways:

● Completely new functions, with new names, can be added to the class.

● Functions from the base class can be replaced by new functions with the same names; these are **overrides**.

When a function in the new class is called from within the program, the system checks first to see if there is a function of that name in the new class. If there is, the function is executed; if there is not, the function in the base class is executed.

CNotebookApp contains one new member function, CNotebookApp, which is **declared** as follows:

```
CNotebookApp();
```

This is the class **constructor**, a function that is called as the CNotebookApp object is being created (i.e. when the application is run). Every class should have a constructor, whose name must be the same as the class name.

You could use this function to carry out initialisation tasks, setting up the application ready for use. However, the function does not return any value; therefore, when it has finished its work you have no way of knowing whether it has been successful. For this reason, C++ introduces a second stage to the initialisation by declaring the following function:

```
virtual BOOL InitInstance();
```

This function has been placed in the Overrides section, indicating that it is an override member function, replacing one of the same name in CWinApp. The 'BOOL' in front of the function name specifies that InitInstance will return a Boolean value: TRUE if the initialisation was successful, otherwise FALSE.

Take note

The 'virtual' keyword ensures that the correct version of the function is called when using pointers to objects. For a more detailed discussion of pointers and virtual functions, see *C++ Made Simple*.

The Implementation section of the header file contains a third member function, OnAppAbout, declared as follows:

```
afx_msg  void  OnAppAbout();
```

This function, which will be called when the user selects Help | About, is part of the application's 'message map': the way in which C++ handles user actions and other events. This section of the file is maintained by one of the Developer Studio's wizards and must not be edited manually. Other member functions will be added as they are required.

Other header files have a similar structure to this file, though each will add functions relevant to its own particular class. The document and view header files are described in Chapter 7.

The main application source file

Corresponding to the application header there is a source file, Notebook.cpp, containing the **definitions** of those member functions that were declared in the header file.

The file starts with a list of #include statements. These statements are replaced with the contents of the header files when the source file is compiled, so that the functions declared in those files can be called from within the source file.

Following on from this is the message map, which is described on page 111.

Class constructor

The next section is the definition of the class constructor, identified by the header line:

```
CNotebookApp::CNotebookApp()
```

The header line for any member function consists of the class name, two colons (::) and the function name. The definition itself – that is, the set of instructions that make up the function – is enclosed in braces ({}). To start with, the function contains comments only. There are no instructions, so the function does nothing. Later, you may want to add instructions that are to be performed when the program is first run (i.e. when the application object is created). However, the most important initialisation code is put in the InitInstance function.

Application object

Having defined the class constructor, the program can now create an object for that class. This is done with the single statement:

```
CNotebookApp    theApp;
```

This statement creates a single object, called theApp, for the class CNotebookApp.

Notebook.cpp

```
// Notebook.cpp : Defines the class behaviors for the application.

#include   "stdafx.h"
#include   "Notebook.h"
#include   "MainFrm.h"
#include   "ChildFrm.h"
#include   "NotebookDoc.h"
#include   "NotebookView.h"

#ifdef _DEBUG
#define  new  DEBUG_NEW
#undef   THIS_FILE
static char THIS_FILE[] = __FILE__;
#endif

/////////////////////////////////////////////////////////////////////
// CNotebookApp

BEGIN_MESSAGE_MAP(CNotebookApp,      CWinApp)
    //{{AFX_MSG_MAP(CNotebookApp)
    ON_COMMAND(ID_APP_ABOUT,       OnAppAbout)
        // NOTE - the ClassWizard will add and remove macros here.
        //     DO NOT EDIT what you see in these blocks of code!
    //}}AFX_MSG_MAP
    // Standard file based document commands
    ON_COMMAND(ID_FILE_NEW,        CWinApp::OnFileNew)
    ON_COMMAND(ID_FILE_OPEN,       CWinApp::OnFileOpen)
    // Standard print setup command
    ON_COMMAND(ID_FILE_PRINT_SETUP,
CWinApp::OnFilePrintSetup)
END_MESSAGE_MAP()

/////////////////////////////////////////////////////////////////////
// CNotebookApp construction
CNotebookApp::CNotebookApp()
{
    // TODO: add construction code here,
    // Place all significant initialization in InitInstance
}

/////////////////////////////////////////////////////////////////////
// The one and only CNotebookApp object
CNotebookApp   theApp;

/////////////////////////////////////////////////////////////////////
// CNotebookApp initialization
BOOL    CNotebookApp::InitInstance()
```

Some generated comments and blank lines have been removed to save space

Include all header files

Message map

Constructor function

Object creation

Initialisation code

```
{
    AfxEnableControlContainer();
    // Standard initialization
#ifdef _AFXDLL
    Enable3dControls();         // Call when using MFC in shared DLL
#else
    Enable3dControlsStatic(); // Linking statically
#endif

    // Change the registry key under which our settings are stored.
    SetRegistryKey(_T("Local   AppWizard-Generated   Applications"));
    LoadStdProfileSettings();  // Load std INI file options (inc MRU)

    CMultiDocTemplate*    pDocTemplate;
    pDocTemplate = new CMultiDocTemplate(
        IDR_NOTEBKTYPE,
        RUNTIME_CLASS(CNotebookDoc),
        RUNTIME_CLASS(CChildFrame), // custom MDI child frame
        RUNTIME_CLASS(CNotebookView));
    AddDocTemplate(pDocTemplate);

    // create main MDI Frame window
    CMainFrame* pMainFrame = new CMainFrame;
    if   (!pMainFrame->LoadFrame(IDR_MAINFRAME))
        return FALSE;
    m_pMainWnd = pMainFrame;

    // Enable drag/drop open
    m_pMainWnd->DragAcceptFiles();

    // Enable DDE Execute open
    EnableShellOpen();
    RegisterShellFileTypes(TRUE);

    // Parse command line for standard shell commands etc.
    CCommandLineInfo   cmdInfo;
    ParseCommandLine(cmdInfo);

    // Dispatch commands specified on the command line
    if   (!ProcessShellCommand(cmdInfo))
        return FALSE;

    // The main window has been initialized, so show and update it.
    pMainFrame->ShowWindow(m_nCmdShow);
    pMainFrame->UpdateWindow();

    return TRUE;
}
```

Change registry key

Create document template

Load the main frame

Command line parameter

Display the window

Class initialisation

The header line for the InitInstance function (which was declared in the CNotebookApp class definition in Notebook.h) is as follows:

```
BOOL    CNotebookApp::InitInstance()
```

In this case, the statement begins with 'BOOL', indicating that the function returns a TRUE or FALSE value. The type of the function here must match the type specified in the header-file declaration. InitInstance is a function of CWinApp, so the version for this class is an override.

Take note

There is no semi-colon (;) at the end of the header line or following the closing brace.

The function definition created by the AppWizard already contains a number of standard instructions, which are worth inspecting. The first statement allows the application to use ActiveX controls; the next block selects 3-D controls. The application is then set up to use the registry.

The registry

Windows 95 applications are registered in the **system registry**. This is a file containing initialisation information about all the applications on a particular computer. Applications created with the MFC use the registry to store all the start-up information that would normally be stored in WIN.INI, SYSTEM.INI or an application-specific INI file. (You can use your own INI file, providing it is held in the application directory, though this is not recommended.)

The SetRegistryKey function makes the connection to the registry; this is the one statement in Notebook.cpp that you should change. Replace the standard text in quotes with your own company (or other) name. For example:

```
SetRegistryKey(_T("Southbury    Software"));
```

This statement will add a section in the registry for your applications; initialisation data can then be stored for each application.

The next instruction loads some of this data:

```
LoadStdProfileSettings();
```

This statement loads the list of most recently used (MRU) files, which appears at the bottom of the File menu.

The document template

MFC applications use three main classes to display a window. The visible portion of the window, including its border, title bar and buttons (control menu, Minimise, Maximise and Close), is controlled by the frame-window class. Everything inside the border (excluding the title bar) is called the window's **client area**; display of data in this area is handled by the view class. The data itself is controlled by the document class.

The **document template** ties these components together. The main class for document templates is CDocTemplate. Two other classes are derived from this: CSingleDocTemplate for SDI applications and (in this case) CMultiDocTemplate for MDI applications. The code in InitInstance defines a pointer to an object of this class:

```
CMultiDocTemplate*    pDocTemplate;
```

The 'new' operator allocates memory for a new object:

```
pDocTemplate = new CMultiDocTemplate(...);
```

The effect of this statement is that pDocTemplate points to the new document template object (in this case, the template for the child windows).

The **parameters** within the brackets determine the objects that are to be linked together by the template:

● The resource identifier for a menu (IDR_NOTEBKTYPE)

● The document class (CNotebookDoc)

● The frame (CChildFrame)

● The view (CNotebookView)

The final statement creates the document template and adds it to a list held by the application object, CNotebookApp:

```
AddDocTemplate(pDocTemplate);
```

Loading the main window

The remaining statements in InitInstance are concerned with loading and displaying the main frame. The first statement defines a pointer to the main frame class an creates an object of that type:

```
CMainFrame* pMainFrame = new CMainFrame;
```

Whereas we had two separate statements for the creation of the document template, here they are combined. The variable pMainFrame is created as a pointer to a new CMainFrame object. The application will attempt to load this new object into memory, using the function:

```
pMainFrame->LoadFrame(IDR_MAINFRAME)
```

This function returns a value of TRUE if the LoadFrame action was completed successfully. The program calls the function, tests the return value and acts on it in a single statement:

```
if(!pMainFrame->LoadFrame(IDR_MAINFRAME))
    return FALSE;
```

The ! operator represents 'not', so this statement may be interpreted as follows: 'If the result of LoadFrame is not TRUE, end InitInstance and return a value of FALSE'.

Command line parameters

If the frame loaded successfully, various options are enabled and the command line is checked for parameters:

```
CCommandLineInfo    cmdInfo;
ParseCommandLine(cmdInfo);
```

The first statements defines an object of the type CCommandLineInfo, called cmdInfo. The ParseCommandLine function extracts any parameters from the command line and stores them in this object. The most useful option is to specify a filename, in which case the corresponding file will be opened when the application is run. (If the parsing fails, InitInstance will also fail, returning a FALSE value.)

Completing the initialisation

The next two statements display the window and, since the program has reached this stage without problem, the final statement returns a value of TRUE.

If the value returned from InitInstance is TRUE, the main window will have been displayed and will be waiting for the user to take some action. A return value of FALSE closes down the application (there will have been a Windows error message box of some sort).

Exercises

1 List the classes in the VisDraw application and identify the base classes in each case.

2 Change the version information for the application, including the Comments and Company Name.

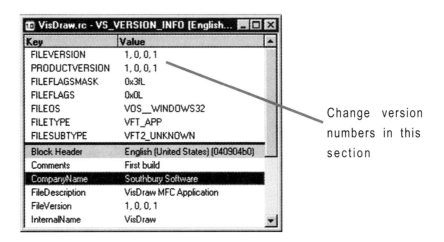

3 Change the registry key for VisDraw.

For solutions to these exercises, see page 175.

4 Dialog boxes

Creating a dialog box

Dialog boxes are an inescapable part of any application. The simplest applications consist of a single dialog box (e.g. the Calculator) but most applications use many such boxes, ranging from a simple 'Save changes?' box to more complicated dialogs, containing many buttons, scroll bars, text boxes and so on.

Dialog boxes are created as resources, objects defined in separate files which can be re-used in other applications. The dialog-box resource is a template, from which Windows creates the dialog-box object itself. You can see the dialog boxes that are currently available to the application by clicking on the ResourceView tab in the Project Workspace window and opening up the Dialog folder.

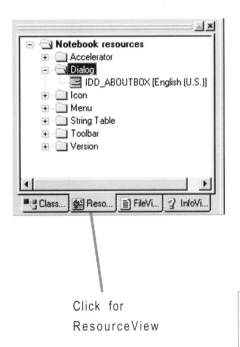

Click for
ResourceView

In the case of SDI and MDI applications you will start with one dialog box, which will display the Help | About information.

Each dialog box must be identified by a unique ID number, represented by an ID name (e.g. IDD_ABOUTBOX).

ID names must consist of letters, numbers and the underscore character: no spaces or other characters. The corresponding ID number is allocated by the system but its value is of no real interest.

Take note

The IDs are defined in Resource.h, where the association between number and name can be inspected — but should not be changed.

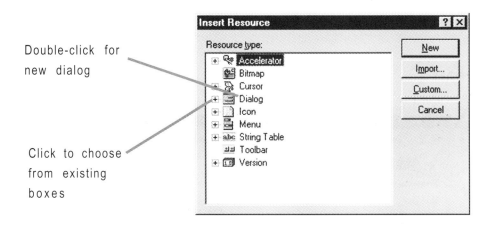

Double-click for new dialog

Click to choose from existing boxes

To create a new dialog box, select Insert | Resource from the Developer Studio menu (or press **[Ctrl-R]**). The Insert Resource dialog box appears, with a list of possible resource types. Double-click on Dialog; a new dialog is displayed.

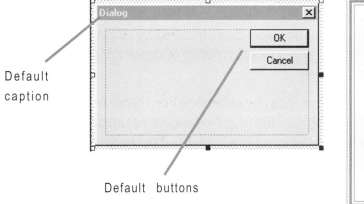

Default caption

Default buttons

Take note

You can also add an existing dialog from another application by opening up the Dialog folder and selecting from the list.

The default dialog box contains two buttons – OK and Cancel – and a title bar (including title and close button). It has also been given a default ID (IDD_DIALOG1), which is added to the dialog resource list.

You should change at least the title and ID. These are two of the dialog's **properties** (items of data which define the appearance and behaviour of the dialog box). To display the properties sheet, click on the new dialog box and then right-click; select Properties from the pop-up menu. (Alternatively, select View | Properties or press **[Alt-Enter]**.)

53

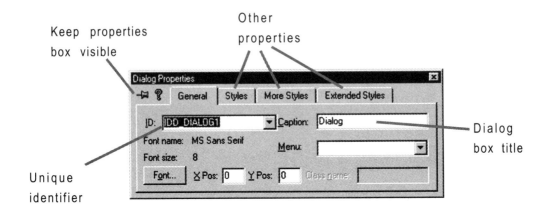

Keep properties box visible

Other properties

Unique identifier

Dialog box title

Change the ID to something more memorable but keeping to the convention that dialog IDs begin with 'IDD_'. Change the Caption (the text on the title bar) to something more meaningful to the user. For example, the ID for a dialog box containing user details could be IDD_USERDETAILS and the Caption could be 'User details'.

Further properties can be viewed or changed by clicking on the other tabs at the top of the Properties box. Most of these are properties that can be turned on or off.

When you save the changes (by selecting File I Save All or clicking on the Save All button), the RC file (e.g. Notebook.rc) and Resource.h file are updated. These files must not be edited manually; always make your changes using the appropriate Developer Studio options.

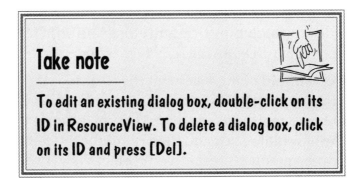

Take note

To edit an existing dialog box, double-click on its ID in ResourceView. To delete a dialog box, click on its ID and press [Del].

The dialog box class

You have now created a new resource but as yet there is no class associated with it; without a class, your application cannot create an object when the dialog box is needed. Most of the work is done for you by the ClassWizard.

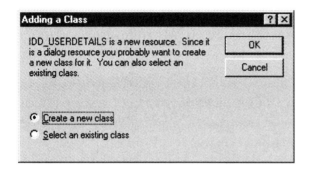

Either select View | ClassWizard or, more simply, press **[Ctrl-W]**. ClassWizard offers to create a new class, so click on OK.

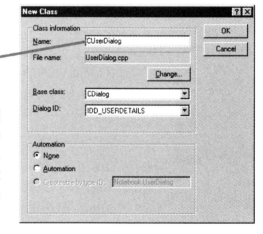

Enter new
class name

ClassWizard displays a dialog box with which you can create the new class. The base class, from which the new dialog box will be derived, is given as CDialog, as you would expect.

Tip

Always start class names with 'C'. It will also be helpful later if you end dialog box class names with 'Dialog'.

All that is required is that you enter a name for the new class (e.g. CUserDialog). ClassWizard will do the rest. The wizard suggests a filename for the source file; when you click on OK, ClassWizard creates source and header files for the new dialog class (e.g. UserDialog.cpp and UserDialog.h).

Finally, the main ClassWizard dialog box is displayed. There is nothing more to be done at this stage, so click on OK.

Dialog box files

The ClassWizard has created two new files for you, a source file and a header file.

Dialog header file

Comparing the header file (UserDialog.h) with the application header (Notebook.h), you will see that there are many similarities and most of the code should be familiar.

The main part of the files is taken up with the class definition. Since CUserDialog is derived from CDialog, all that is needed are any new or overridden functions. There is a constructor, also called CUserDialog, though this time the function has a parameter:

```
CUserDialog(CWnd* pParent = NULL);
```

The variable pParent points to the window (of type CWnd) that owns the dialog box (i.e. the window that is active when the dialog box is created). In this case, the variable is set to NULL, indicating that the parent window is the main application window.

The Dialog Data section sets up variables for use with the dialog box.

There is no InitInstance function (all initialisation work can be done in the constructor, since the dialog box returns a TRUE or FALSE value when it closes). However, there is a DoDataExchange function, which handles the transfer of data between the program and the dialog box (for a full explanation, see page 96).

Finally, there is no member function in the Implementation section, since we have not yet added any functionality to the box.

Tip

To view the header file, double-click on the class name in ClassView. To view the source file, double-click on the dialog itself in the editor window.

UserDialog.h

```
// UserDialog.h : header file
//

#if      !defined(AFX_USERDIALOG_H__BF8E5AC1_..._INCLUDED_)
#define      AFX_USERDIALOG_H__BF8E5AC1_..._INCLUDED_

#if _MSC_VER >= 1000
#pragma  once
#endif // _MSC_VER >= 1000
```

Some blank lines and comments have been omitted; conditional directives have also been abbreviated.

```
/////////////////////////////////////////////////////////////////////////
// CUserDialog dialog

class CUserDialog : public CDialog
{
// Construction
public:
    CUserDialog(CWnd* pParent = NULL);    // standard constructor

// Dialog Data
    //{{AFX_DATA(CUserDialog)
    enum { IDD = IDD_USERDETAILS };
        // NOTE: the ClassWizard will add data members here
    //}}AFX_DATA

// Overrides
    // ClassWizard generated virtual function overrides
    //{{AFX_VIRTUAL(CUserDialog)
    protected:                              // DDX/DDV support
    virtual void DoDataExchange(CDataExchange* pDX);
    //}}AFX_VIRTUAL
```

Member function to get data

```
// Implementation
protected:

    // Generated message map functions
    //{{AFX_MSG(CUserDialog)
        // NOTE: the ClassWizard will add member functions here
    //}}AFX_MSG
    DECLARE_MESSAGE_MAP()
};
```

No functions yet

```
//{{AFX_INSERT_LOCATION}}
// Microsoft Developer Studio will insert additional declarations
// immediately before the previous line.

#endif   //   !defined(AFX_USERDIALOG_H__BF8E5A..._INCLUDED_)
```

UserDialog.cpp

```cpp
// UserDialog.cpp : implementation file
//


#include  "stdafx.h"
#include  "Notebook.h"
#include  "UserDialog.h"

#ifdef  _DEBUG
#define  new  DEBUG_NEW
#undef  THIS_FILE
static char THIS_FILE[] = __FILE__;
#endif
```

> Constructor will be expanded later

```cpp
///////////////////////////////////////////////////////////////////////////
// CUserDialog dialog


CUserDialog::CUserDialog(CWnd*   pParent   /*=NULL*/)
    : CDialog(CUserDialog::IDD,  pParent)
{
    //{{AFX_DATA_INIT(CUserDialog)
        // NOTE: the ClassWizard will add member initialization here
    //}}AFX_DATA_INIT
}


void   CUserDialog::DoDataExchange(CDataExchange*   pDX)
{
    CDialog::DoDataExchange(pDX);
    //{{AFX_DATA_MAP(CUserDialog)
        // NOTE: the ClassWizard will add DDX and DDV calls here
    //}}AFX_DATA_MAP
}
```

> Data exchange functions will be added later.

> Message map will be extended later

```cpp
BEGIN_MESSAGE_MAP(CUserDialog,      CDialog)
    //{{AFX_MSG_MAP(CUserDialog)
        // NOTE: the ClassWizard will add message map macros here
    //}}AFX_MSG_MAP
END_MESSAGE_MAP()


///////////////////////////////////////////////////////////////////////////
// CUserDialog message handlers
```

Dialog source file

The source file (UserDialog.cpp) is very short, as nothing much has been added to the basic dialog functionality provided by CDialog. (It is easy to forget that there is a huge amount of source code tucked away in CDialog and the other MFC classes.)

The constructor is empty and DoDataExchange does nothing but call the corresponding function in CDialog. These functions will be expanded later by ClassWizard.

The source file ends with a message map (see page 111).

The About dialog box

If you now open up Notebook.cpp and take a look at the CAboutDlg section at the end of the file, its contents should be clearer. This section combines all the code that you have just inspected in the new dialog's header and source files (leaving aside the #include and #if statements, which appear at the top of Notebook.cpp). The file includes everything needed to create a class for the About dialog box and implement it.

The first part of the code defines the class, CAboutDlg, and corresponds exactly to Notebook.h. Following that, there are definitions for the constructor and DoDataExchange, and the message map. The code ends with the function that actually displays the dialog box (described next).

Take note

The code may seem complicated but ClassWizard sets it all up for you – all you need do is link the dialog into your program.

Displaying the dialog box

You have now created a template for a dialog box, currently containing just two buttons, and a corresponding class. The next stage is to combine the template and class to create a dialog object, when required.

The compiler must be able to recognise the class name and its member functions when the main application file is compiled. Therefore, you need to include the dialog header file in Notebook.cpp by adding an extra #include line at the top of the file:

```
#include    "NotebookDoc.h"
#include    "NotebookView.h"
#include "UserDialog.h"    // New include line
```

At this point, assume that the User Details dialog box is to be displayed at the start of the program (for instance, to check the user's password). The dialog box must be created when all the initialisation work has been done but before the user can take any action; therefore the necessary code is added to the end of InitInstance.

The code comes immediately after the statements that display the main window (so the dialog box will be displayed over the top of the window). The first line creates the dialog box object (an instance of CUserDialog, in a variable called dlg):

```
CUserDialog    dlg;
```

CDialog has a member function, DoModal, which is inherited by CUserDialog and which displays the dialog box. A function is invoked by specifying the object and function, separated by a full stop.

Tip

To edit the function, either display the source file with FileView and scroll down to the function, or jump straight to the function by selecting InitInstance() from the CNotebookApp folder in ClassView.

Display dialog

```
BOOL    CNotebookApp::InitInstance()
{
        // First part of InitInstance is unchanged
    ...
    // The main window has been initialized, so show and update it.
    pMainFrame->ShowWindow(m_nCmdShow);
    pMainFrame->UpdateWindow();

    // Add new code here, replacing original 'return TRUE' statement
    CUserDialog  dlg;
    if (dlg.DoModal() == IDOK)
    {
        // OK pressed - check password
        return TRUE;     // if password correct
    }
    else
    {
        // Cancel pressed
        return  FALSE;
    }
}
```

Therefore the new instance of this class can display the box with the following statement:

```
dlg.DoModal()
```

When the dialog is displayed, the user has two choices: click on OK or click on Cancel. These buttons are set up so that they close the dialog box and DoModal returns a value to the calling function of either IDOK or IDCANCEL, depending on which button was pressed. The return value can be tested with a statement in the form:

```
if (return-value == IDOK)
{
    // OK statements
{
else
}
    // Cancel statements
}
```

Take note

The DoModal function does everything needed: displays the box, waits for a button press, removes the box and passes back a result.

61

If the example as it currently stands, the return value from the dialog box ends the InitInstance function is one of two ways:

● If OK is pressed, the return value is IDOK and the function ends, returning a TRUE value. The main application then continues as before.

● If Cancel is pressed, the return value is IDCANCEL, so the 'else' clause is invoked; the function ends and returns a FALSE value. This closes down the application.

Since one of these actions must occur, the original 'return TRUE' statement is redundant and should be removed.

Try this out by executing the application again (press **[Ctrl-F5]** and confirm that the files are to be rebuilt). The dialog box will pop up over the main window, with OK and Cancel respectively continuing or ending the application.

Displaying the About dialog box

The last function in Notebook.cpp uses a simpler version of this code to display the About dialog box when the user selects Help | About:

```
void    CNotebookApp::OnAppAbout()
{
    CAboutDlg   aboutDlg;
    aboutDlg.DoModal();
}
```

Here, there is no interest in the DoModal return value, so there is no test or subsequent action. The 'void' on the first line indicates that the OnAppAbout function does not return a value.

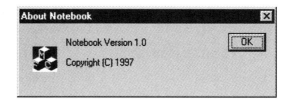

Dialog-based applications

Dialog-based applications do not have the complexities of SDI and MDI applications, as they do not have to display windows. This becomes obvious when you compare the sample dialog-based application (ScrapPad) with the MDI application (Notebook).

Application files

The header files are almost identical, but ScrapPad.h has no OnAppAbout member function (as this application has no menu bar).

The source files are also similar but ScrapPad.cpp has none of the code for creating documents and views, nor does it include the code for accessing the registry or parsing the command line (there are no data files to load).

The ShowWindow and UpdateWindow functions are replaced by the code below, which displays the main dialog box. In this case the return value from the DoModal function is stored in an integer variable, nResponse:

```
int nResponse = dlg.DoModal();
```

This is necessary because we need to deal with three possible outcomes: OK clicked, Cancel clicked or the box being closed by some other event (an error, for instance).

The 'if' statement provides locations for writing code to deal with the button clicks.

At the end of the function, the 'return FALSE' statement passes back a FALSE value regardless of the button that was clicked. By this stage, the main dialog box will have been closed down one way or another, so there is nothing more to be done in the application (and therefore a return value of TRUE would be meaningless).

Take note

This single statement performs three tasks: creating an integer variable, nResponse; executing the DoModal function; and assigning the result to nResponse.

Dialog InitInstance

```
BOOL    CScrapPadApp::InitInstance()
{
    AfxEnableControlContainer();

    // Standard initialization
    // If you are not using these features and wish to reduce the size
    //   of your final executable, you should remove from the following
    //   the specific initialization routines you do not need.

#ifdef _AFXDLL
    Enable3dControls();    // Call this when using MFC in a shared DLL
#else
    Enable3dControlsStatic();
                          // Call this when linking to MFC statically
#endif

    CScrapPadDlg  dlg;
    m_pMainWnd = &dlg;
    int nResponse = dlg.DoModal();

    if (nResponse == IDOK)
    {
        // TODO: Place code here to handle when the dialog is
        //   dismissed with OK
    }
    else if (nResponse == IDCANCEL)
    {
        // TODO: Place code here to handle when the dialog is
        //   dismissed with Cancel
    }

    // Since the dialog has been closed, return FALSE so that
    // we exit the application, rather than start the application's
    // message pump.

    return  FALSE;
}
```

Display dialog and test result

Code to be added depending on outcome

Dialog files

The dialog-based application also has two files for the main dialog box itself (in this example, ScrapPadDlg.h and ScrapPadDlg.cpp).

Comparing ScrapPadDlg.h with UserDialog.h, you will see that the only significant difference is the inclusion of an icon declaration and five member functions in the Implementation section.

```
protected:
    HICON   m_hIcon;
    // Generated message map functions
    //{{AFX_MSG(CScrapPadDlg)
    virtual  BOOL  OnInitDialog();
    afx_msg  void  OnSysCommand(UINT  nID,  LPARAM  lParam);
    afx_msg  void  OnDestroy();
    afx_msg  void  OnPaint();
    afx_msg  HCURSOR  OnQueryDragIcon();
    //}}AFX_MSG
    DECLARE_MESSAGE_MAP()
```

The source file has the standard CAboutDlg definition. (In this case, the About box is accessed from the main dialog box's control-menu button.) The file also contains the definitions of the additional functions, which are called when particular events occur. Event handling is discussed in Chapter 6.

From this point on, the handling of dialog boxes and applications is the same, whether you are using an SDI/MDI application or a dialog-based application.

Take note

All the dialog boxes we have considered so far are **modal** boxes: they must be closed before the user can work with the main application. Modeless dialog boxes (such as Word's Find dialog), which stay open when you click on the main window, are more complicated and rarely needed — see the C++ Help for more details.

Exercises

1 Create a dialog box for the VisDraw application. Change its ID to IDD_LINESDIALOG and give it a title of 'Line-drawing features'. (This dialog will be used for setting line widths.)

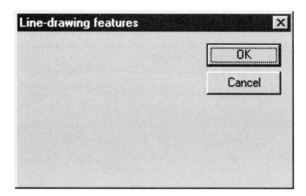

2 Create a class for the dialog, calling it CLinesDialog.

3 Test the dialog box by displaying it as soon as the application is run.

For solutions to these exercises, see page 175.

5 Dialog controls

Adding controls

The client area of any dialog box (the area inside the borders and below the title bar) contains one or more **controls**. These are the objects that display information or allow the user to perform actions: for example, text labels, command buttons, edit boxes, scroll bars and icons.

You can add any combination of controls to a dialog box but remember that when the application is run the user will be free to click, double-click or drag the controls in any order and at any time (subject to the restrictions you impose at design time). You will have to add member functions for those events that you want to handle (see Chapter 6).

To add controls, open the Dialog folder in ResourceView and double-click on the ID of your dialog box. The dialog box is displayed in the editor window, with the Control palette next to it. This palette contains the controls you can add to the box.

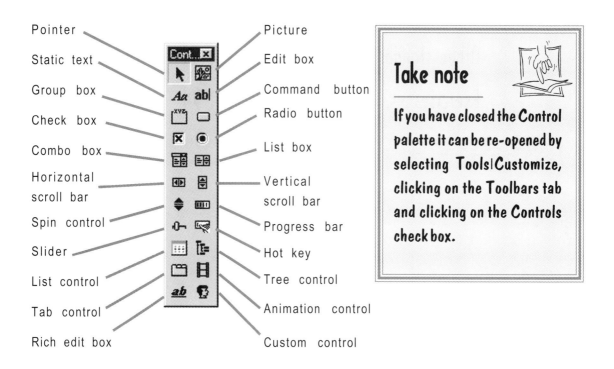

Pointer
Static text
Group box
Check box
Combo box
Horizontal scroll bar
Spin control
Slider
List control
Tab control
Rich edit box

Picture
Edit box
Command button
Radio button
List box
Vertical scroll bar
Progress bar
Hot key
Tree control
Animation control
Custom control

Take note

If you have closed the Control palette it can be re-opened by selecting Tools|Customize, clicking on the Toolbars tab and clicking on the Controls check box.

A control is added in one of two ways:

● Click on the control in the palette and then click on the dialog box; a standard-sized control appears at that point.

● Click on the control then mark out a rectangle by dragging over the dialog box; the control fills the rectangle.

You can change a control by clicking on it. The editor draws a wide border, containing 'sizing handles', around the edge of the control. You now have the following options:

● Drag a sizing handle to change the size and shape of the control.

● Drag from inside the control border to move the control.

● Press **[Del]** to delete the control.

You can change the size of the dialog box by dragging its sizing handles.

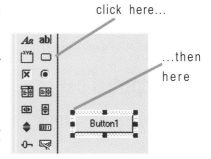

To add a button, click here...

...then here

Button1

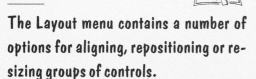

Tip

The Layout menu contains a number of options for aligning, repositioning or resizing groups of controls.

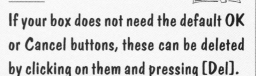

Tip

If your box does not need the default OK or Cancel buttons, these can be deleted by clicking on them and pressing [Del].

The Control palette includes the standard controls but you can also use other, third-party controls – known as **ActiveX** controls (which replace OLE controls and VBX controls). These controls are generally more sophisticated.

You can add an ActiveX control by clicking on the dialog box and then right-clicking. Select Insert ActiveX Control from the pop-up menu and then choose a control from the list.

Control properties

The behaviour and appearance of a control is determined by its **properties**. These are data values which, for any particular object, specify details such as size, position, colour, text and valid user actions.

The properties are different for each type of control (though there are some properties that are common to all or most controls). The value of a particular property is its **setting**, and this can of course be different for each instance of the control (e.g. two buttons will have different pieces of text displayed on their surface). Each new instance of a control starts with a default setting for each property; most of these will be acceptable, so you need change only those property settings that are inappropriate.

The properties box

The properties for a control are viewed and changed using a Properties dialog box. Click on the control, then right-click. From the pop-up menu, select the Properties option. The dialog box is displayed.

The properties that are included will depend on the type of control; the settings for the properties will match the particular instance of the control that is currently selected. If you click on a different control and then select Properties again, the settings will be displayed for that control.

Tip

You can keep the Properties box visible by clicking on the 'pin' icon in the top left of the box.

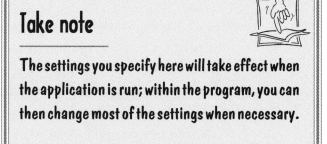

Take note

The settings you specify here will take effect when the application is run; within the program, you can then change most of the settings when necessary.

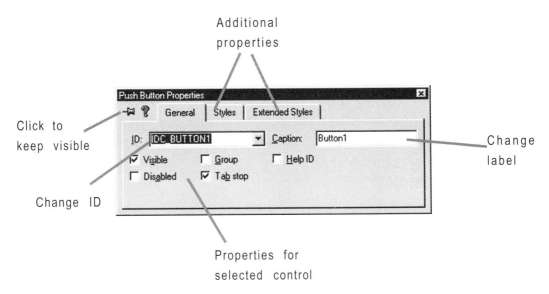

Additional properties

Click to keep visible

Change ID

Change label

Properties for selected control

The Properties box usually has more than one tab, giving you access to additional groups of properties. However, the most important properties for a control (and the ones you are most likely to change) are shown on the first tab.

For each control on the dialog box, you should change at least the ID and Caption (see below).

Multiple controls

You can select a group of controls in the following ways:

- Hold down **[Shift]** and then click on two or more controls. Each time you click on a new control, it is identified by blue sizing handles (and the other controls' handles turn white).

- Move the pointer to a blank area of the form and then drag over the controls. Any control wholly covered by the marked rectangle is selected.

- A control can be removed from the group by holding down **[Shift]** and clicking on the control again.

Any change made to the property settings will apply to all the selected controls. Some properties (such as the ID) will be greyed out, and can only be changed for a single control. You can also drag the group of controls to a new position.

Common properties

Some properties are common to all or most controls; for instance, all controls have an ID and most have a Caption. The most useful properties are described here. Each control has additional properties, specific to that type of control; for example, only the edit box has a Password property (allowing the box to be used for the entry of passwords). Additional properties are described for each type of control later in this chapter.

Control ID

Every control has an **ID**, which identifies the control in the code (for instance, when passing values to the control at run time). Each new control is given a default name, starting with 'IDC_'. This name should be changed to something more meaningful (even for controls that you think you are unlikely to use in a function).

The naming rules are as follows:

- IDs can be up to 247 characters long (though you should keep them much shorter than this!)

- IDs can consist of letters, numbers and underscore(_) characters; no other characters or spaces are allowed.

- IDs must start with a letter or underscore character.

- Upper and lower case are treated as being the same but the MFC convention is to use all capitals (as the IDs represent constants).

- IDs must be unique within the application (though you can define a symbol name and apply it to similar controls in several dialog boxes).

You should also follow the MFC convention of starting all control IDs with 'IDC_' and dialog IDs with 'IDD_'. It is also a good idea to include the control type: e.g. IDC_BUTTON for buttons, IDC_EDIT for text boxes.

Caption and access keys

Most controls have a **Caption** (the most notable exception being the edit box). This holds the text that is displayed on the control. There are no restrictions on the caption; this is purely cosmetic text.

Including an & in front of a character in the Caption denotes that character as an access key. The control can then be 'clicked' by pressing **[Alt]** and the access key together. The access key is underlined in the Caption when the program is run.

Normally, the first character is underlined but if that character has already been used as an access key in another control on the same dialog box, any other character can be selected. If two controls have the same access key, pressing that key with **[Alt]** selects each in turn. (This practice should be avoided.)

Edit boxes do not have a Caption. (Text typed by the user is held in the Text property.) Therefore they cannot be given an access key directly. To get round this problem, a static label control should be placed next to the edit box and given an access key; the access key for the label (which cannot be clicked itself) acts as an access key for the following edit box. The label must come immediately before the edit box in the tab order (see below).

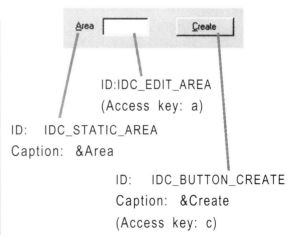

ID:IDC_EDIT_AREA
(Access key: a)

ID: IDC_STATIC_AREA
Caption: &Area

ID: IDC_BUTTON_CREATE
Caption: &Create
(Access key: c)

Size and position

The size of a control is changed by dragging the sizing handles on the corners and edges of the control. Similarly, the control's position on the dialog box is changed by dragging from within the control.

The size and position of the selected control are shown in two boxes on the right of the status bar. The first box gives the position of the control relative to the top left-hand corner of the dialog box; the second gives the width and height of the control.

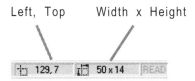

All measurements are given in DLUs (dialog box units). Horizontally, one DLU is a quarter of the average width of a character in the dialog box font. The physical size of a control therefore varies from one computer to another, rather than being a fixed size in inches, centimetres or pixels.

When resizing or repositioning a control you can use the rulers at the top and left of the dialog editor window to judge the distances. Alternatively, you can switch the **grid** on; the corners of the controls will then 'snap' to grid points, making it easier to line up controls. The rulers and grid are turned on and off by clicking icons on the Dialog toolbar (which starts off docked at the bottom of the editor window).

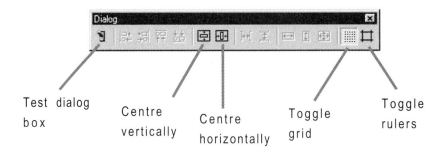

When the grid is switched on, grid points are displayed (these disappear when the program is run). By default, the grid points occur every 5 DLUs but this can be changed with Layout | Guide Settings.

The Dialog toolbar also contains buttons for centring a control either vertically or horizontally in the dialog box.

If you select a group of controls, other options become available on the toolbar (for instance, to align the controls on the left of the dialog box or make them all the same height). These buttons correspond to options in the Layout menu.

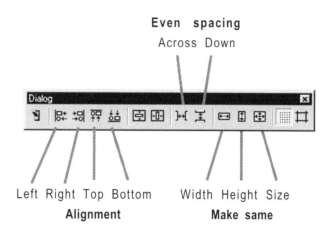

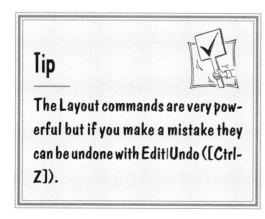

Tip

The Layout commands are very powerful but if you make a mistake they can be undone with Edit|Undo ([Ctrl-Z]).

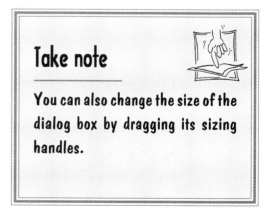

Take note

You can also change the size of the dialog box by dragging its sizing handles.

Tab stops and focus

When the user clicks on a window, the window is said to have the focus: that is, it is the current window. The current window is identified by the fact that its title bar is a different colour. Only one window can have the focus at any time.

Similarly, one (and only one) control in the window has the focus. In most cases, this is indicated by a thicker border, by highlighting or by the appearance of a flashing cursor.

When the user presses the **[Tab]** key, the focus moves from one control to the next. The **Tab stop** property determines whether or not the control can receive the focus. If it cannot (the Tab Stop box is not checked in the Properties box), the focus will skip to the next control.

The order in which the focus moves from one control to the next is determined by the **tab order**, which is changed with Layout | Tab Order (or by pressing **[Ctrl-D]**). The dialog box is displayed, with a number shown for each control, indicating its position in the tab order.

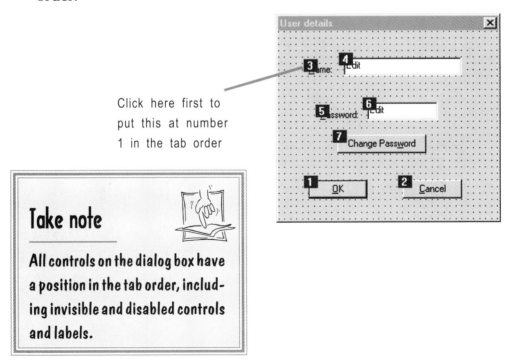

Click here first to put this at number 1 in the tab order

Take note

All controls on the dialog box have a position in the tab order, including invisible and disabled controls and labels.

To change the tab order:

● If you want to change the order for all controls, click on them in the order you require. Remember to include all controls (even those with Tab Stop turned off). Those that already have the correct tab number must be clicked at the appropriate point, otherwise they will change position.

● If you want to change the order of just some of the controls, start by holding down **[Ctrl]** and clicking on the control before the first to be changed. Then click on the remaining controls in the required order.

When the changes have been made, click on a blank part of the dialog box. Remember to save the changes after any major change.

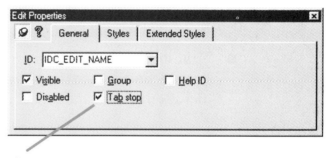

Turn Tab Stop on to allow
control to receive the focus

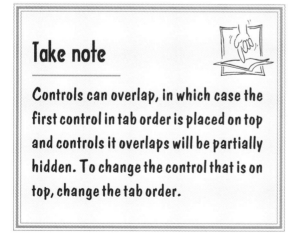

Take note

Controls can overlap, in which case the first control in tab order is placed on top and controls it overlaps will be partially hidden. To change the control that is on top, change the tab order.

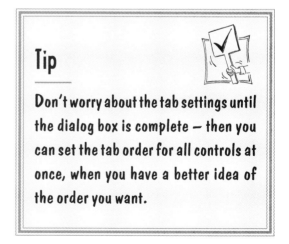

Tip

Don't worry about the tab settings until the dialog box is complete – then you can set the tab order for all controls at once, when you have a better idea of the order you want.

Groups

By default, you can move about on the dialog box using the cursor-control keys, which take you through the controls in tab order. The Down and Right arrow keys move you forwards in the tab order while Up and Left take you backwards.

You can split the controls into groups using the **Group** property. If a control has Group switched on, it is the first control in the group. All controls following form part of the group, up to the next control in tab order with the Group switched on. (This control forms the start of the next group.)

The following points should be noted:

● Labels have their Group property switched on by default; labels always form the start of a new group.

● You can move into an edit box using the arrow keys but you cannot move out in this way, even if it is part of a group.

● If the first control in tab order has Group switched off, it will form part of the group at the end of the tab order (i.e. you can move between the last and first controls using the arrow keys).

Help ID

The **Help ID** property, when checked, indicates that you want the system to generate a unique help ID for the control. This ID is used when setting up context-sensitive help.

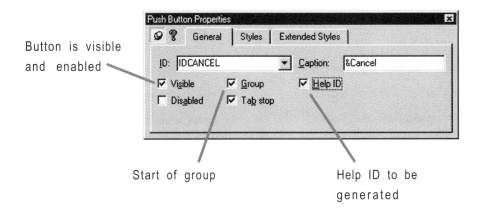

Button is visible and enabled

Start of group

Help ID to be generated

Visible and Disabled

The **Visible** property determines whether the control can be seen; **Disabled** determines whether it can be used. As a rule, it is less confusing for the user if components are always visible but not necessarily enabled.

When a control is disabled (its Disabled property is checked), any text displayed on it is greyed out and clicking on the control has no effect. If a control is not visible (its Visible property is not checked), the user obviously cannot click on it and therefore its Disabled property is irrelevant.

For example, if there is a 'Save' button on the dialog box the Disabled property may be switched on until data is entered or changed at which point the Disabled property would be switched off by the program. The alternative would be for the Save button to be invisible until the data changed, when Visible would be turned on; however, this would be disconcerting for the user.

The Visible option is particularly useful where the value of one component affects the applicability of others. For instance, a set of radio buttons may allow you to choose between different types of membership. One part of the dialog box may contain labels and edit boxes that change, depending on the selection; these would all exist as separate controls but only those that are applicable would be made visible. Another use of the Visible property would be to make additional options or information available when a command button is clicked.

Standard controls

Visual C++ includes a number of standard controls on the Control palette. Many more are available as ActiveX controls, selected from Insert ActiveX Control on the dialog editor's pop-up menu. The standard controls, and their more useful properties, are described here.

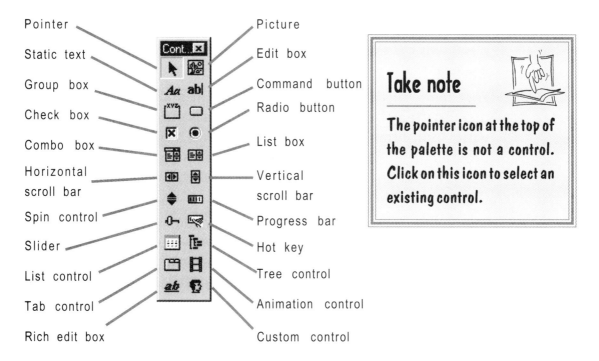

Pointer
Static text
Group box
Check box
Combo box
Horizontal scroll bar
Spin control
Slider
List control
Tab control
Rich edit box

Picture
Edit box
Command button
Radio button
List box
Vertical scroll bar
Progress bar
Hot key
Tree control
Animation control
Custom control

Take note

The pointer icon at the top of the palette is not a control. Click on this icon to select an existing control.

Command buttons

Command buttons are used for performing actions. A function is attached to each command button and is executed when the user clicks on the button. You cannot decide the order in which buttons are clicked but you do have full control over the action taken once the user has clicked a button.

The text that appears on the top of the button is held in the Caption property. For long captions, switch on the Multi-line property (in the Styles tab); the text can then wrap over more than one line (though you will need to increase the height of the button). The position of the text on the button is determined by the **Horizontal alignment** and **Vertical alignment** properties.

The **Icon** and **Bitmap** properties allow you to replace the text on the button by an icon or bitmap (see Chapter 8).

The Default button property identifies the button that is activated when users press the **[Enter]** key; usually this is the OK button. Each dialog box may have only one default button.

Static text controls

The **static text** control adds text labels to a dialog box: titles, user instructions, text for edit boxes and so on. The user cannot click on this type of control but you may change the text itself at run time; for example, after selecting a file the label text can be changed to display the filename.

The text is held in the Caption property. The horizontal position of the text in the rectangle marked out for the static control is determined by the **Align text** property; Left, Center or Right (by default, the left). The **Center vertically** property centres the text between the top and bottom; if this property is not checked the text appears at the top of the label area.

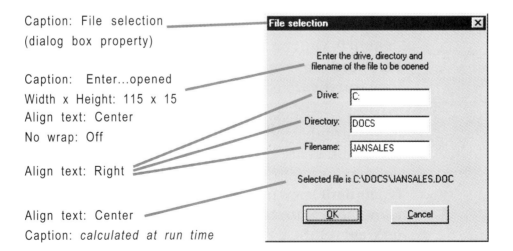

Caption: File selection
(dialog box property)

Caption: Enter...opened
Width x Height: 115 x 15
Align text: Center
No wrap: Off

Align text: Right

Align text: Center
Caption: *calculated at run time*

File selection

Enter the drive, directory and
filename of the file to be opened

Drive: C:

Directory: DOCS

Filename: JANSALES

Selected file is C:\DOCS\JANSALES.DOC

OK   Cancel

By default, long items of text wrap over from one line to the next. You can stop this happening by turning on the **No wrap** property (which has the opposite effect to the command button's Multi-line property). If No Wrap is on, text that is too long for the label area is truncated to fit. Alternatively, switching on the **Simple** property aligns the text to the left and does not allow wrapping but does not truncate the text.

The **Sunken** property gives a sunken effect while **Border** draws a box around the edge of the label area.

The **No prefix** property treats & as a normal character, rather than the indicator of an access key. This is useful when you don't know what the contents of the label will be (for instance, when displaying a filename or text entered elsewhere by a user).

Edit boxes

abl

The edit box control provides the simplest method for the user to enter data. When the edit box has the focus, a vertical cursor is displayed and the user can make an entry, using all the usual Windows editing features.

The user's entry is held in the control's Text property, which cannot be changed at design time. You can convert the entry to all upper case or all lower case letters with the **Uppercase** and **Lowercase** properties respectively. The **Number** property restricts entries to the digits 0-9. You can also mask the user's entry by switching on the **Password** property; all characters are displayed as asterisks (*) as they are typed.

To allow larger quantities of text to be typed, switch on Multi-line and increase the height of the box. The **Alignment** property may then be set to Left, Centered or Right. Text will wrap at the end of the line unless you switch on **Auto HScroll**, in which case the user continues typing until a new paragraph is started by pressing **[Ctrl-Enter]**. To allow the user to start new paragraphs by pressing **[Enter]**, switch on **Want return**. If Want Return is off, pressing **[Enter]** activates the dialog box's default button; otherwise, this button is activated only when the user moves out of the edit box and presses **[Enter]**.

For multi-line boxes, turn on the Vertical scroll property if you want the user's text to continue beyond the bottom of the box. If Auto HScroll is on, you should also turn the **Horizontal scroll** property on, so that users can see their position in the text.

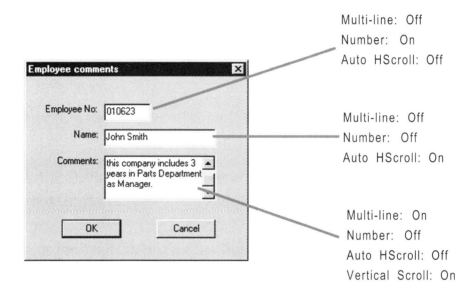

The **Border** property (which is on by default) draws a box around the edit area.

For more sophisticated text entry, use the Rich Edit control. This allows you to make use of a wide range of text-formatting facilities. However, there is quite a bit of programming to be done to link the control into the various rich-edit classes. See the Visual C++ WORDPAD sample application for details.

Radio buttons and check boxes

Radio buttons and check boxes provide two standard methods for the user to make choices.

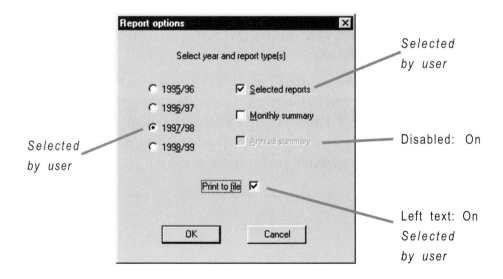

Radio buttons usually appear in groups of two or more. All buttons on the form are interrelated (unless they are in a frame – see page 85). The control consists of circle with a piece of text next to it. When the user clicks a radio button, a black circle is added; only one button can be selected at a time, so any other selected button is cleared.

The text for the button is held in the Caption property and most of the other properties relate to the appearance of the radio button:

- **Left text** puts the text to the left of the button, rather than the right.

- **Push-like** and **Flat** change the appearance of the button itself.

- **Multi-line** allows multi-line text.

- **Icon** and **Bitmap** replace the text with an icon or bitmap.

- **Horizontal alignment** and **Vertical alignment** change the position of the text within the text area.

The Auto property should usually be left switched on, as this affects the automatic selection of one button from the set.

Check boxes work in a similar way to radio buttons, the main difference being that the check boxes on a dialog box operate independently of each other. When the user clicks on a check box a tick is added to it; there is no effect on other check boxes. Clicking again clears the check box. As a result, the user may select several boxes at the same time – or no boxes.

Properties for check boxes are similar to those for radio buttons. There is an additional property, **Tri-state**, which gives the check box three states: clear, checked and greyed. Each time the user clicks on the check box, the box changes from one state to the next.

Tip

To make a check box temporarily unavailable, switch on its Disabled property. It is less disconcerting for the user then for it to disappear completely.

Take note

Radio buttons and check buttons are created from the same class as command buttons, CButton. Their different appearance and behaviour is determined by the value of the Button Style property.

Frames

 If you need more than one group of radio buttons on a dialog box you must first add a frame to the box. Frames are also useful if a box contains a large number of controls and you want to group them together for neatness.

Frames are added to the dialog box by drawing a rectangle around the area to be enclosed. The controls that are to be displayed inside the frame can then either be dragged into the frame (if they exist) or be created inside the frame.

Frames have no effect on the operation of the dialog box; they are purely cosmetic. If the frames are to be used for grouping radio buttons, the buttons must first be put into sequential tab order. The first button in the frame must then have its Group property switched on. Repeat this process for any other groups of radio buttons.

The Caption for the frame is the piece of text in the top left-hand corner.

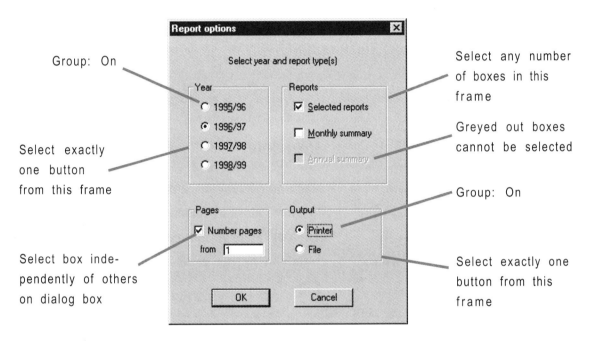

Group: On

Select exactly one button from this frame

Select box independently of others on dialog box

Select any number of boxes in this frame

Greyed out boxes cannot be selected

Group: On

Select exactly one button from this frame

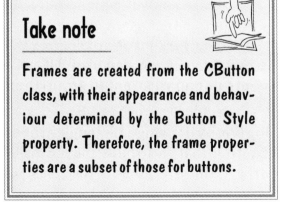

Take note

Frames are created from the CButton class, with their appearance and behaviour determined by the Button Style property. Therefore, the frame properties are a subset of those for buttons.

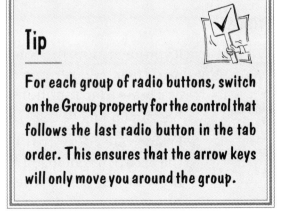

Tip

For each group of radio buttons, switch on the Group property for the control that follows the last radio button in the tab order. This ensures that the arrow keys will only move you around the group.

Lists

Two types of standard control are provided for selecting items from a list: list boxes and combo boxes.

The **list box** allows the user to select from a list of options. The box consists of a rectangle containing a list of items, with a vertical scroll bar on the right (which appears only when the list is too long to fit in the box). The width and height of the box are determined by the shape of the control you add to the dialog box. The contents of the list are set at run time (see Chapter 6).

The **Selection** property specifies the way in which the user can select items from the list:

Single   Only one item can be selected.

Multiple   Several items can be selected by clicking on them (clicking again removes them).

Extended   As for Multiple but the selection can be extended by dragging.

None   No selection can be made.

The **Sort** property (if selected) sorts the contents of the list box into alphabetical order. **Multi-column** allows the list box to have more than one column (with the number of columns set at run time).

The **Horizontal scroll** and **Vertical scroll** properties add scroll bars, when needed. **Disable no scroll** displays a greyed out vertical scroll bar when the list is not long enough to fill the box.

No integral height, if selected, keeps the size of the list box to that set when the box was created; if the list does not fit an exact number of items, only part of the item at the bottom of the list will be visible. Otherwise, the height of the box will be adjusted at run time so that it fits an exact number of items.

A **combo box** is a combination of a list box and an edit box. An item can be selected from the list by clicking on an item (as for list boxes) or by typing part of a name in the edit box section. Depending on the type of combo box, the user may be able to type new values that are then added to the list.

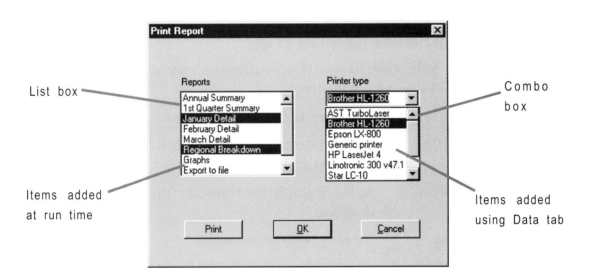

List box

Items added
at run time

Combo
box

Items added
using Data tab

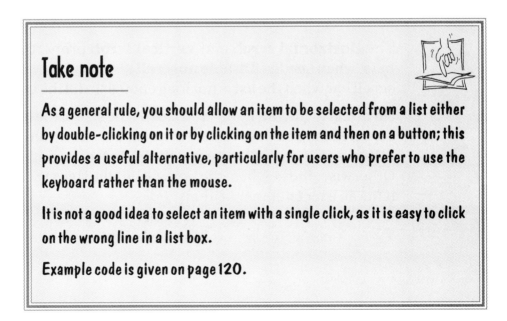

Take note

As a general rule, you should allow an item to be selected from a list either by double-clicking on it or by clicking on the item and then on a button; this provides a useful alternative, particularly for users who prefer to use the keyboard rather than the mouse.

It is not a good idea to select an item with a single click, as it is easy to click on the wrong line in a list box.

Example code is given on page 120.

88

The way the combo box works is determined by the **Type** property (in the Styles tab). The property may take the following settings:

Simple   The list is visible at all times. An item can be selected by clicking on it or typing in the edit box.

Dropdown   The list is displayed when the user clicks on the arrow button. An item can then be selected by clicking or by typing in the edit box.

Drop List   The list is displayed by clicking on the arrow. An item can be selected only be clicking on it.

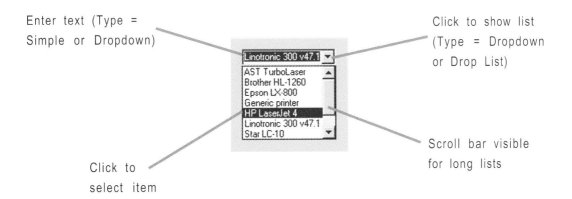

Enter text (Type = Simple or Dropdown)

Click to show list (Type = Dropdown or Drop List)

Scroll bar visible for long lists

Click to select item

Other properties are a mixture of those for list boxes and edit boxes.

The contents of the list for a combo box can be added at design time using the Data tab. Items should be typed into the empty list box, using **[Ctrl-Enter]** to start a new line for each item.

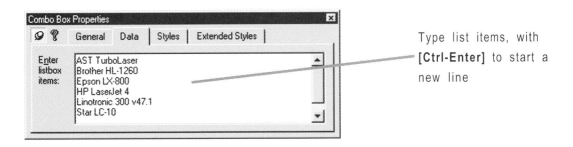

Type list items, with **[Ctrl-Enter]** to start a new line

Combo boxes are useful when you want to give the user the option of adding new items. Drop-down boxes also take up less space on the dialog box than simple lists.

 The **List control** provides a variation of the simple list box, with each item in the list consisting of a bitmap and a label rather than straight text. Setting up such a list is rather more complex, as it requires you to manage a bitmap list structure in the program (see *CListCtrl* and *Working with a List Control* in Visual C++ Help).

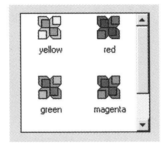

Other standard controls

The control palette includes a number of other controls, which are used less frequently and require more complex procedures to set up:

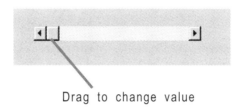

- The **horizontal scroll bar** gives you a 'floating' scroll bar. The user can move the square block on the bar and the program can then convert this into a value.

Drag to change value

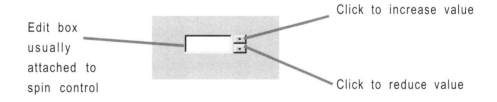

- The **vertical scroll bar** provides a 'floating' scroll bar in the other direction.

- The **spin control** is usually attached to an edit box and allows you to increase or decrease the corresponding value by clicking on its up and down arrows.

Edit box usually attached to spin control

Click to increase value

Click to reduce value

- The **progress bar** provides a more sophisticated way than a horizontal scroll bar for displaying the proportion of some activity that has been completed.

Bar shows proportion of activity completed

- The **slider** gives you another way of choosing from a range of values (and is more pleasant to look at than a scroll bar).

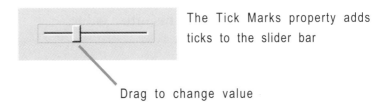

The Tick Marks property adds ticks to the slider bar

Drag to change value

- The **hot key** control allows the user to press specific key combinations to perform corresponding procedures.

- The **tree control** gives you a hierarchical list, in which 'nodes' can be expanded or collapsed and items selected (working in a similar way to the directory list on the left of Windows Explorer).

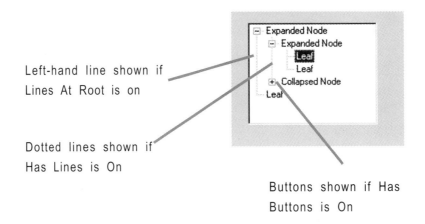

Left-hand line shown if Lines At Root is on

Dotted lines shown if Has Lines is On

Buttons shown if Has Buttons is On

- The **tab control** lets you fit more information on a dialog box by storing the controls on a number of tabs, only one of which is visible at any time.

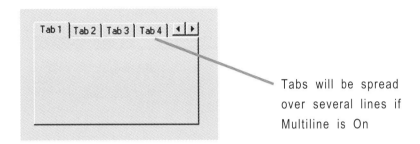

Tabs will be spread over several lines if Multiline is On

- The **animation** control allows you to display video clips in standard AVI format.

Examples of these controls can be found in the Visual C++ help files.

Exercises

1   Add controls to the Line-Drawing Features dialog box in VisDraw, as shown below. The combo boxes should not be sorted; the boxes will be filled at run time. The top label should be centred within a wide area (this label will be extended at run time). Test the dialog box and save it.

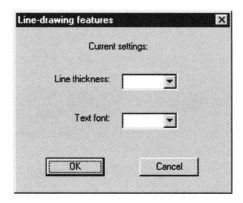

2   Add controls to the VisCalc dialog box, as shown below. The first two edit boxes should allow numeric entries only. Run the application to test it.

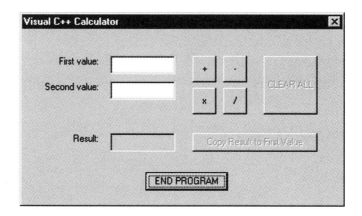

For solutions to these exercises, see page 176.

6 Events and functions

Connecting variables

The dialog resource that has been created has everything it needs for the dialog box to operate successfully: title bar, borders, buttons and controls. All the standard functionality of this dialog box is inherited from the CDialog class. Nothing more has to be done for the dialog controls to act as you would expect.

Associated with this resource is a dialog class, to which will be added all the extra functionality that you need. The dialog controls store data (such as the entry in an edit box or the state of a radio button) and you will need to change or make use of this data. However, you cannot access the control values directly. The problem now is to transfer data between the dialog controls and the program. This is solved by the Visual C++ **Dialog Data Exchange** (DDX) mechanism.

DDX is a process whereby member variables in the program are connected to corresponding controls and data can flow freely between the two. Most of the processes are hidden from you and the hard work of setting up the mechanism is done for you by ClassWizard.

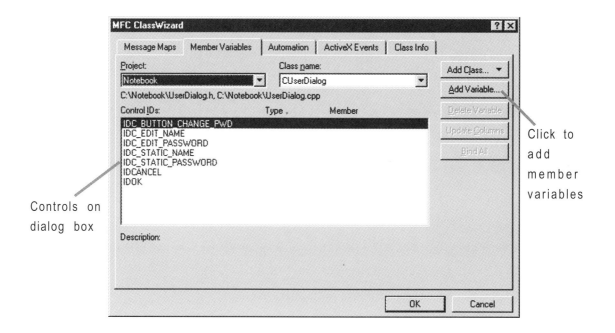

Controls on dialog box

Click to add member variables

Adding member variables

Call up ClassWizard by pressing **[Ctrl-W]** and click on the Member Variables tab (see previous page).

The IDs for the controls on the dialog box are listed. You can create member variables corresponding to any of these controls but should only create those that you will need. Click on a control ID and then on Add Variable. The Add Member Variable dialog box is displayed.

Enter variable name

Change type if necessary

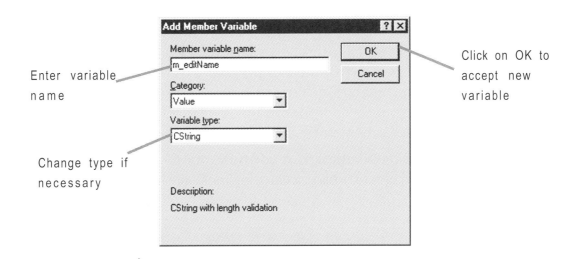

Click on OK to accept new variable

Enter a variable name, following the usual rules. ClassWizard suggests 'm_' as a starting point and you should add to this. Choose a name that is close to the control ID; it's a good idea to start the name with an abbreviation representing the control type (e.g. m_editName for the IDC_EDIT_NAME control).

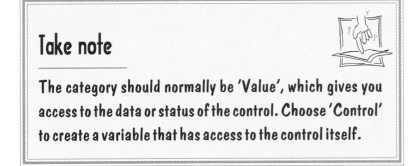

Take note

The category should normally be 'Value', which gives you access to the data or status of the control. Choose 'Control' to create a variable that has access to the control itself.

In some cases you have a choice of types for the variable. For instance, for edit boxes the type can be CString (the normal choice) or a selection of numeric and other types.

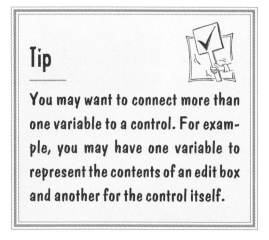
When you click on OK, the ClassWizard Member Variables list is redisplayed. It now shows the member variables that have been created, with their types.

For some variables, you can add validation options. The options are shown at the bottom of the box when the variables are highlighted. For strings, you can specify the maximum length of the string; for numbers, you can restrict the values entered to a particular range. So, for an edit box, you might decide to limit the entry to a fixed number of characters (remembering that the control's properties already allow you to restrict the entry to upper or lower case letters). In the example below, the Password edit box is restricted to eight characters.

All validation is handled for you by Visual C++; if the user attempts to make an invalid entry, a warning message is displayed.

Selected member variable

Limit length of entry

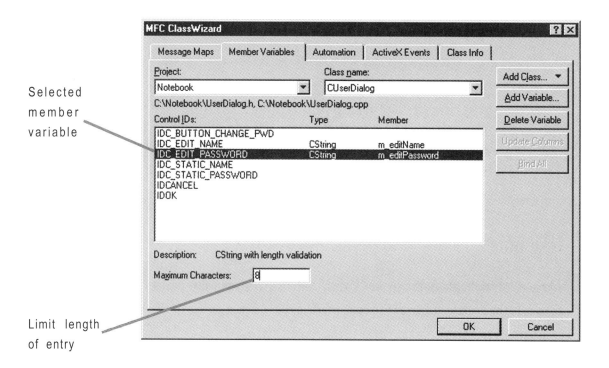

Using the member variables

These variables can now be used within your program. In the example below, the last part of the CNotebookApp::InitInstance function from Notebook.cpp has been modified to test the password entered in the User Details dialog box.

The new code starts by giving a value to m_editName. When the dialog box is displayed, this value will be copied to the corresponding edit control and displayed as a default value.

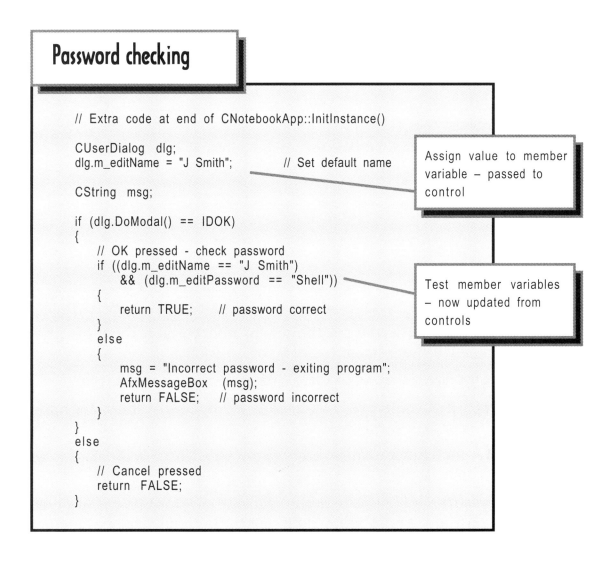

Password checking

```
// Extra code at end of CNotebookApp::InitInstance()

CUserDialog  dlg;
dlg.m_editName = "J Smith";              // Set default name

CString  msg;

if (dlg.DoModal() == IDOK)
{
    // OK pressed - check password
    if ((dlg.m_editName == "J Smith")
        && (dlg.m_editPassword == "Shell"))
    {
        return TRUE;     // password correct
    }
    else
    {
        msg = "Incorrect password - exiting program";
        AfxMessageBox  (msg);
        return FALSE;    // password incorrect
    }
}
else
{
    // Cancel pressed
    return  FALSE;
}
```

Assign value to member variable – passed to control

Test member variables – now updated from controls

When the dialog box is closed by clicking on OK, the values of the two edit boxes are copied back to the corresponding member variables, m_editName and m_editPassword. (No extra code had to be added to effect this transfer.) The program then tests the variables against constant values, to see if the password is correct; in a fully-functional version of this program the program would test more than one user name and would read the passwords from an encrypted file.

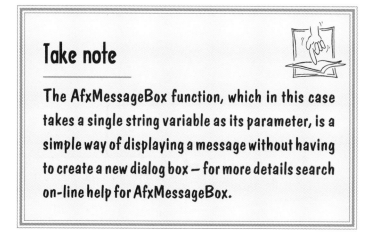

Take note

The AfxMessageBox function, which in this case takes a single string variable as its parameter, is a simple way of displaying a message without having to create a new dialog box – for more details search on-line help for AfxMessageBox.

Dialog box produced by AfxMessageBox

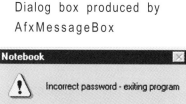

DDX code

The ClassWizard has added several pieces of code to your files in order to carry out the data transfer.

In the dialog header file, the new member variables have been declared (in the example, two new string variables).

In the dialog source file, ClassWizard has made two changes:

- The member variables have been initialised in the dialog box's constructor function.

- DDX and DDV functions have been added to the DoDataExchange function.

When the DoModal function is invoked it calls the UpdateData function from CWnd. This function calls the DoDataExchange function from the Dialog box being opened. The DoDataExchange function takes as its parameter a pointer to a CDataExchange object; the function in turn calls the DDX functions for the controls for which data is to be transferred. Each function takes as its parameters the pointer to the CDataExchange object, the control ID and the member variable. There are different DDX functions for different types of variable.

When the OK button is clicked a function called OnOK is called; this function also calls UpdateData, though this time the data is transferred the other way.

Tip

The Cancel button does not transfer data automatically. If you want to check control values before the program closes you must call UpdateData explicitly.

Take note

The DoDataExchange function also includes a DDV function for each validation check you set up. This function displays a warning if the controls tries to pass back an invalid value.

If you want to change the values of controls while the dialog box is in use, or make use of changed values, then you must call UpdateData from within the code. The function takes a Boolean value as its parameter:

● UpdateData(FALSE) transfers data from the member variables to the dialog controls.

● UpdateData(TRUE), or just UpdateData(), transfers data from the dialog to the member variables.

Some examples of this function are given later in this chapter.

Data exchange declarations

```
class CUserDialog : public CDialog
{
// Construction
public:
    CUserDialog(CWnd* pParent = NULL);    // standard constructor

// Dialog Data
    //{{AFX_DATA(CUserDialog)
    enum { IDD = IDD_USERDETAILS };
    CString   m_editName;
    CString   m_editPassword;
    //}}AFX_DATA


// Overrides
    // ClassWizard generated virtual function overrides
    //{{AFX_VIRTUAL(CUserDialog)
    protected:
    virtual void DoDataExchange(CDataExchange* pDX);
                                      // DDX/DDV support

    //}}AFX_VIRTUAL

// Implementation
protected:

    // Generated message map functions
    //{{AFX_MSG(CUserDialog)
        // NOTE: the ClassWizard will add member functions here
    //}}AFX_MSG
    DECLARE_MESSAGE_MAP()
};
```

New member variables declared

Declaration of data exchange function

Take note

You should always use ClassWizard to add new member variables, as you will then be sure that the declaration and initialisation have been completed correctly.

Tip

If you want to give a default value to an edit box, amend the initialisation code so that there is a piece of text between the double quotes.

Data exchange implementation

```
CUserDialog::CUserDialog(CWnd*    pParent    /*=NULL*/)
    :  CDialog(CUserDialog::IDD,  pParent)

{
    //{{AFX_DATA_INIT(CUserDialog)
    m_editName  =  _T("");
    m_editPassword  =  _T("");
    //}}AFX_DATA_INIT
}

void    CUserDialog::DoDataExchange(CDataExchange*    pDX)
{
    CDialog::DoDataExchange(pDX);
    //{{AFX_DATA_MAP(CUserDialog)
    DDX_Text(pDX,    IDC_EDIT_NAME,    m_editName);
    DDX_Text(pDX,    IDC_EDIT_PASSWORD,    m_editPassword);
    DDV_MaxChars(pDX,    m_editPassword,    8);
    //}}AFX_DATA_MAP
}

BEGIN_MESSAGE_MAP(CUserDialog,        CDialog)
    //{{AFX_MSG_MAP(CUserDialog)
        // NOTE: the ClassWizard will add message map macros here
    //}}AFX_MSG_MAP
END_MESSAGE_MAP()
```

Member   variables
initialised

DDX   and   DDV   functions
added

Take note

The _T() function maps a piece of text onto the appropriate
character set for the system in which the program is being
compiled. This means that your program can be transported to
other platforms without requiring changes. For ASCII-based
systems, _T() has no effect. If you think you may compile under
non-ASCII systems, you should place all constant text in a _T()
function; otherwise, this precaution can be ignored.

The event-led environment

In traditional programming languages, the programmer remains in absolute control when the program is run. The program consists of a linear sequence of coded instructions, with branches to particular points in the program. At each stage of the program, the user is offered a limited number of options and the program branches to the relevant section of code, according to the choice that has been made. If the code has been written correctly, there should be no surprises.

Windows programming languages, such as Visual C++, start from a completely different viewpoint. At any one time there will be many objects on the screen: dialog boxes, command buttons, menus, edit boxes and so on. The user is free to click, drag or type on any object and, in most circumstances, is not constrained to follow a linear path through a fixed sequence of actions.

This event-led environment requires the programmer to take a completely new approach. Rather than trying to confine the user to a limited number of actions, the programmer must create a program that reacts correctly, whatever the user does. This is not as daunting as it sounds; there are, of course, ways of limiting the user's scope (for example, making dialog boxes and controls invisible or greying out check boxes) but the simplest solution is to do nothing.

For each object on the screen there are a number of possible **events**. Some of these are generated by the user: for instance, clicking or double-clicking on the mouse button, dragging the object or pressing a key. Others occur as a result of some other event: for example, a window opening or closing, or a component getting or losing the focus.

Whenever an event occurs, the affected object generates one or more **messages**. Each message has a name, and this usually gives some idea of what event has occurred; for example, the BN_CLICKED message is generated by a button when it is clicked. Each message name represents an integer and Windows has a long list of #define statements to link them together.

The code to respond to these messages is contained in special Visual C++ functions called **message handlers**. Each object has its own set of message handlers. Theoretically, you could create a message handler for every message but in practice you will only fill in the handlers for those events that are of interest.

For example, a command button's events include being clicked and double-clicked; for an edit box, events include getting and losing the focus, the text being changed, a scroll bar being clicked or the input text being truncated. However, you may only want to provide code for one event (such as the command button's Click event); any other events would be ignored.

Each event results in some action being taken by Windows itself. For instance, clicking on a command button causes the button to change its appearance while the mouse button is held down; clicking on a window's Minimise button reduces the window to an icon. In these cases, you cannot alter the object's behaviour but you can add to it; for example, you may activate a new dialog box when the command button is clicked or display a message when a window is minimised.

Therefore, the next task, after creating the user interface, is to decide the events that are to be handled and create the appropriate functions.

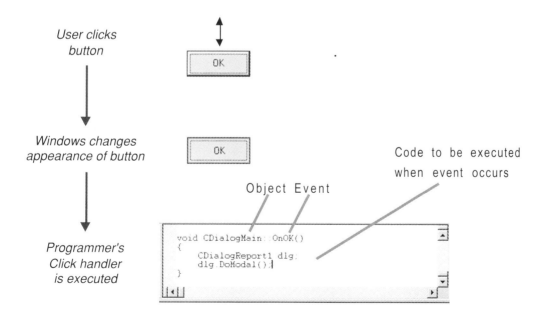

Adding message handlers

Message handlers can be added with little difficulty. Display the dialog box and double-click on the control that is to be given a handler. A new dialog box is displayed.

Messages for which handlers can be created

Existing handlers (none at present)

Description of event

Control (or dialog) currently selected

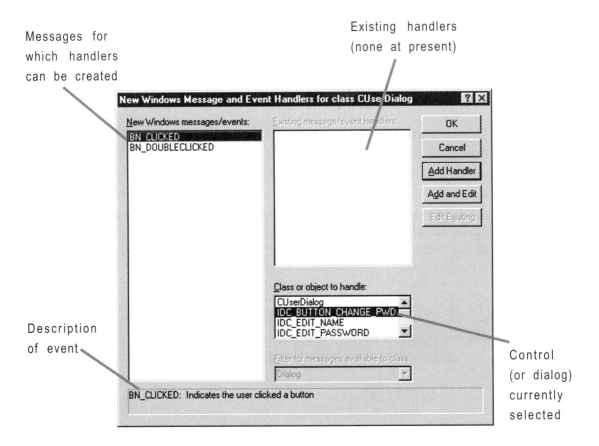

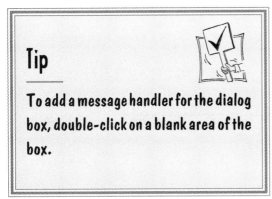

Tip

To add a message handler for the dialog box, double-click on a blank area of the box.

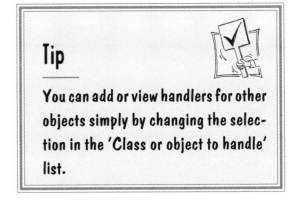

Tip

You can add or view handlers for other objects simply by changing the selection in the 'Class or object to handle' list.

The list box in the middle of the dialog box shows all the objects for which you can add handlers: the dialog box and its controls. The control that was double-clicked is highlighted.

Corresponding to the selected object, the main list on the left of the dialog box shows all the messages that can be handled. For instance, for a command button the messages are called BN_CLICKED and BN_DOUBLECLICKED, representing the click and double-click events respectively.

When you have added a handler, it will appear in the third list box.

Creating the event-based function

There are two options for adding a message handler:

- Click on Add Handler to add a function, then add the handler code later.
- Click on Add and Edit to add a function and fill in the code straight away.

When you click on a message and then Add and Edit, you are asked to supply a name for the new function.

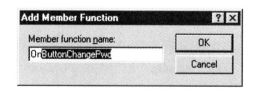

107

In most cases, the name consists of the word 'On' plus the event and the object name (with underscores removed and the name converted to upper and lower case letters). For example, the suggested handler name for the EN_VSCROLL message (indicating the user clicked the vertical scroll bar) for the edit box with an ID of IDC_EDIT_PASSWORD will be OnVscrollEditPassword.

As a general rule, you should accept the default name.

Visual C++ then adds an empty function to the bottom of the dialog box's source file (in the Message Handlers section). All that this function contains is a comment, reminding you to add the appropriate code.

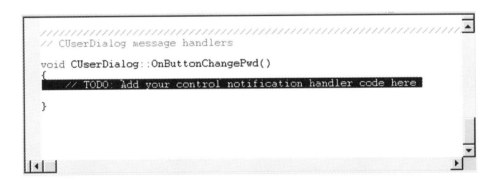

```
////////////////////////////////////////////////////////////////////////
// CUserDialog message handlers

void CUserDialog::OnButtonChangePwd()
{
        // TODO: Add your control notification handler code here

}
```

Take note

When the handler has been added, double-clicking on the control takes you to the handler code.

The example above shows the Click event for the Change Password button (IDC_BUTTON_CHANGE_PWD) on the User Details dialog box (class CUserDialog). This has been added to UserDialog.cpp.

Filling in the handler code

You can now add any standard C++ code to this function. In the example below, the New Password button on the User Details dialog box now has a handler that calls up another dialog box, where the password can be changed. The handler is declared as follows:

```
void    CUserDialog::OnButtonChangePwd();
```

Before compiling the program you must create the New Password dialog box and generate a class for it (CDialogNewPwd). The header file for this dialog must then be included at the top of UserDialog.cpp.

When the button is clicked, the first task is to update the member variables with the current contents of the edit boxes. This is done using the UpdateData() function. (Only the standard OK button has this facility built in, so it is very easy to forget this stage and wonder why the program does not seem to be getting the correct data.)

The handler next checks that the correct password has been entered; you do not want to give the opportunity to change the password until you know that an authorised user has logged on! (As before, in a fully-functioning program the password would not be hard-coded but would be read from an encrypted file.) There is no need to specify 'dlg.' here because the member variables have been defined at the top of the program.

If the password is correct, the handler creates the new dialog object (PwdDlg, of type CDialogNewPwd) and executes its DoModal function. Control now passes to the New Password dialog box and returns only when the dialog is closed (the dialog object being destroyed in the process).

If the password has not yet been entered or is incorrect, a warning message is displayed. This time, there is no Return statement, so the User Details dialog box remains on screen for the user to try again.

Change Password handler

```cpp
// UserDialog.cpp : implementation file
//

#include "stdafx.h"
#include "Notebook.h"
#include "UserDialog.h"
#include "DialogNewPwd.h"    // ADD NEW DIALOG HEADER HERE

#ifdef _DEBUG
#define new DEBUG_NEW
#undef THIS_FILE
static char THIS_FILE[] = __FILE__;
#endif

/////////////////////////////////////////////////////////////////
// CUserDialog dialog

CUserDialog::CUserDialog(CWnd*  pParent  /*=NULL*/)
    : CDialog(CUserDialog::IDD, pParent)

{
    //{{AFX_DATA_INIT(CUserDialog)
    m_editName = _T("");
    m_editPassword = _T("");
    //}}AFX_DATA_INIT
}


void  CUserDialog::DoDataExchange(CDataExchange*  pDX)
{
    CDialog::DoDataExchange(pDX);

    //{{AFX_DATA_MAP(CUserDialog)
    DDX_Text(pDX,  IDC_EDIT_NAME,  m_editName);
    DDX_Text(pDX,  IDC_EDIT_PASSWORD,  m_editPassword);
    DDV_MaxChars(pDX, m_editPassword, 8);
    //}}AFX_DATA_MAP
}


BEGIN_MESSAGE_MAP(CUserDialog,    CDialog)
    //{{AFX_MSG_MAP(CUserDialog)
    ON_BN_CLICKED(IDC_BUTTON_CHANGE_PWD,
        OnButtonChangePwd)
    //}}AFX_MSG_MAP
END_MESSAGE_MAP()
```

Include new dialog header

Member variable definitions

Data exchange and validation functions

Message map for handler

```
/////////////////////////////////////////////////////////////////////////////
// CUserDialog message handlers

void    CUserDialog::OnButtonChangePwd()
{
    //Update member variables from controls
    UpdateData();

    // Check to see if password has been entered correctly
    if ((m_editName == "J Smith") && (m_editPassword == "Shell"))
    {
        CDialogNewPwd    PwdDlg;
        PwdDlg.DoModal();       // password correct, so load dialog
    }
    else
    {
        CString  msg;
        msg = "Please enter correct password first";
        AfxMessageBox   (msg);
    }
}
```

Message handler

Message maps

When you click on a button a corresponding function is executed. This seems simple enough but Windows is doing a great deal of work to handle these events when they occur. Almost all of the code that ensures the correct function is executed for each event is hidden from view. The part that you can see consists of the message map that ClassWizard inserts and maintains in your code.

Tip

ClassWizard takes full responsibility for the message maps – don't try editing them yourself.

The dialog box's header file contains the declarations of the message handlers for the dialog class:

```
// Generated message map functions
//{{AFX_MSG(CUserDialog)
afx_msg  void  OnButtonChangePwd();
//}}AFX_MSG
DECLARE_MESSAGE_MAP()
```

In this example, the function OnButtonChangePwd is declared. The comments above and below allow ClassWizard to identify the messages handled by the class; these comments must not be changed and you must not change the functions between them in any way. The DECLARE_MESSAGE_MAP statement is a macro that is expanded during compilation (and declares variables and functions for use in message handling).

The source file contains the message map itself:

```
BEGIN_MESSAGE_MAP(CUserDialog,      CDialog)
   //{{AFX_MSG_MAP(CUserDialog)
   ON_BN_CLICKED(IDC_BUTTON_CHANGE_PWD,
      OnButtonChangePwd)
   //}}AFX_MSG_MAP
END_MESSAGE_MAP()
```

The message map is enclosed in a pair of macros and the functions are listed between special ClassWizard comments. These statements will be expanded during the compilation. Each function in the map identifies the event that is being handled, the control to be monitored and the function to be executed.

As you add more functions using ClassWizard the message map will be expanded.

Using ClassWizard directly

The message handler above was created by double-clicking on the control. You can also set up message handlers directly through ClassWizard. Press **[Ctrl-W]** and click on the Message Maps tab.

This display box has similar components to the one described above but there are a few differences:

● The message handlers that have been created are listed at the bottom of the dialog box. In each case, the corresponding control and message are shown.

● Messages for which there are handlers are printed in bold in the Messages box.

- For the dialog box object, the messages include all the virtual functions, inherited from the base class (CDialog), which can be overridden by new functions.

In the example, the DoDataExchange virtual function has been overridden, so is shown in bold with 'V' next to it in the Member Functions list.

Messages for which
handlers can be created

Objects
for class

Existing
handlers

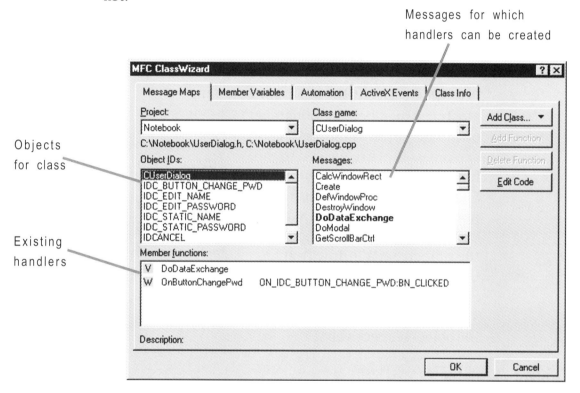

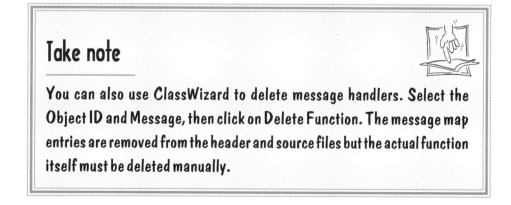

Take note

You can also use ClassWizard to delete message handlers. Select the Object ID and Message, then click on Delete Function. The message map entries are removed from the header and source files but the actual function itself must be deleted manually.

Class member functions

Each class contains a number of **class member functions**. These are built-in functions, which can be executed from within an event-driven function or a user-written member function. The class member functions are used for performing some action on objects based on the class. For instance, every class derived from CWnd has member functions called **MoveWindow** to change the size and position of the object, **SetWindowText** to change the caption text (if the object has any) and **ShowWindow** to display or hide the object. There are many more member functions and each derived class adds its own class members. Many of these functions are used for changing the settings of properties while the program is running.

Most class member functions take one or more **parameters**. These are values that are passed to the function for use within the code. For example, MoveWindow has parameters that set the X and Y co-ordinates, width and height of the object; SetWindowText has the new text as a parameter; and ShowWindow takes values of TRUE or FALSE to show or hide the object respectively.

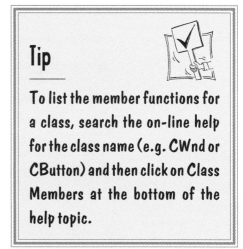

Tip

To list the member functions for a class, search the on-line help for the class name (e.g. CWnd or CButton) and then click on Class Members at the bottom of the help topic.

Control variables

In order to use these member functions, you need to create some additional member variables. This time, the member variables will represent the objects themselves, so are given a Category of 'Control'. Press **[Ctrl-W]** to invoke the ClassWizard, click on the control ID and then on Add Variable. Enter a name for the new variable and select its Category as 'Control'; the variable type is shown as the class name (e.g. CStatic). When you click on OK the new variable is added to the member variables list. Note that you can have more than one variable for each control (for instance, a static label can have variables of type CString and CStatic).

You can now call any of the class member functions using a statement in the form:

variable.function(*parameters*);

For example, if a button has a control member variable called m_CbtnNext the button can be hidden with the statement:

m_CbtnNext.ShowWindow(FALSE);

Calling ShowWindow with a parameter of TRUE redisplays the button.

In some cases, this gives us two ways to perform the same tasks. For example, suppose that a static control is to be used to display the current drive letter. It is connected to two member variables: m_staticDrive (of type CString) and m_CstaticDrive (of type CStatic). The text of the label can be updated by changing the CString variable and then updating the dialog box:

m_staticDrive = "C:";
UpdateData(FALSE);

Alternatively, the label's caption can be updated directly using the CStatic variable and the SetWindowText member function:

m_CstaticDrive.SetWindowText("C:");

In this second case, there is no need to initialise the member variable.

Take note

Remember that when you add a 'value' member variable, ClassWizard will insert a line of initialisation code in the dialog constructor. The specified value in the constructor will replace the default value given in the Properties box. Therefore you must amend the initialisation code to give the variable a string value. For instance, if static labels are connected to member variables (so that they can be changed in the program), they must be initialised with non-blank values, otherwise they will disappear when the program is run.

Getting information from objects

Class member functions can also be used to interrogate their objects. For instance, the GetWindowText function passes the current value of the control's caption to a string. The following code takes the text from one label and redisplays it in a second:

```
CString  msg;
m_Cstatic1.GetWindowText(msg);
m_Cstatic2.SetWindowText("Label text is " + msg);
```

Other functions return the state of the object. For instance, **IsZoomed** tells you whether or not a window is maximised and **IsWindowVisible** returns a TRUE value if the window or control is visible.

Suppose that a dialog box has an edit box and a 'Save Data' button. The following function is called when the edit box loses the focus:

```
void     CDialogLists::OnKillfocusEditData()
{
    CString  msg;
    m_CeditData.GetWindowText(msg);
    if (msg == "")
    {
        m_CbtnSaveData.EnableWindow(FALSE);
    }
    else
    {
        m_CbtnSaveData.EnableWindow(TRUE);
        m_CbtnSaveData.SetFocus();
    }
}
```

The edit box and button have member variables of type 'Control', which are called m_CeditData and m_CbtnSaveData respectively. The contents of the edit box is retrieved using GetWindowText and stored in the CString variable, msg. The contents of this variable are tested. If the box is empty, the button is disabled (by invoking EnableWindow with a parameter of FALSE); otherwise, the button is enabled and gets the focus (by a call to its SetFocus function).

User-defined functions and variables

Although much of the program's work will be done within the event-driven procedures, using member variables connected to controls, you will need to add your own functions and variables for more general options.

User-defined functions

User-defined functions within a class will be required to perform general actions that are needed by more than one event-driven function. It is also more convenient sometimes to take a chunk of code out of an event function and put it in a function of its own.

To add a new function to a class:

1. Click on ClassView in the Project Workspace window.

2. Right-click on the class where the function is to be added (e.g. the dialog box class) and click on Add Member Function. A new dialog box is displayed.

3. Enter 'void' as the Function Type, enter a name in the Function Declaration box, and click on Protected.

4. Click on OK.

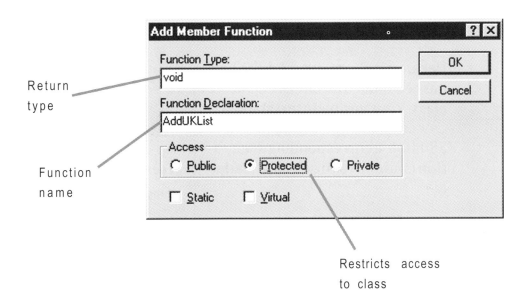

The **Function Type** determines the type of any value returned by the function. For instance, type BOOL would result in the function returning a value of TRUE or FALSE; type 'void' means that the function returns no value.

The **Function Declaration** is where you type the function name; this is the name that appears in the declaration in the header file. (For more complex variables, such as arrays, more information is needed here.)

The **Access** type is one of the following:

Public   The function is accessible from anywhere in the program.

Protected   The function can be called from member functions of the same class or any class derived from that class.

Private   The function can be accessed only by member functions of the same class.

When you click on OK, the new function is added to the end of the source file. This will be an empty function in the form:

```
void    CDialogSelect::AddUKList()
{
}
```

Here, a function called AddUKList has been added to the CDialogSelect class. You can now insert standard C++ code between the braces. In addition, a corresponding declaration is added to the class's header file:

```
protected:
        void AddUKList();
```

This appears in the Implementation section, above the message map.

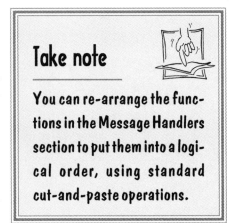

Take note

You can re-arrange the functions in the Message Handlers section to put them into a logical order, using standard cut-and-paste operations.

Local and global variables

If you need local variables, that exist only while a function is being executed, these are added by including a standard C variable declaration within the function. For example:

```
int IndexNum;
```

This statement declares a variable of type integer, called IndexNum, which will exist only while the function is being processed.

For **global variables**, where the value of the variable can be accessed from any function in the class, the variable is added as follows:

1. Click on ClassView.

2. Right-click on the class where the variable is to be added and click on Add Member Variable. A dialog box is displayed.

3. Fill in the variable type and name, and click on Protected (to make the variable available throughout the class and derived classes).

4. Click on OK.

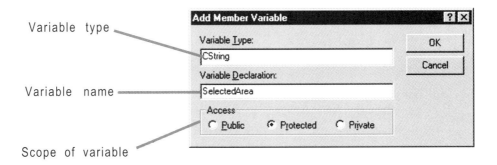

A declaration is added to the Implementation section of the header file. For example:

```
CString SelectedArea;
```

This variable can now be accessed by any member function in the class.

List box example

The following example demonstrates the use of message handlers, class member functions, user-defined functions and member variables.

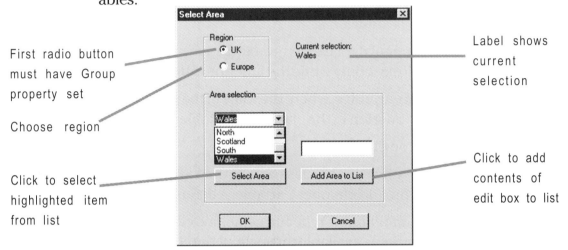

First radio button must have Group property set

Choose region

Click to select highlighted item from list

Label shows current selection

Click to add contents of edit box to list

The dialog box has two radio buttons, a static label, a combo box, an edit box, two extra command buttons (as well as the standard OK and Cancel) and two frames (for appearance only). Four member variables have been attached to the controls:

m_comboArea   A variable of type CComboBox attached to the combo box control itself (for performing operations on the combo box)

m_editNewArea   A variable of type CEdit attached to the edit control (so that we can use the edit box's member functions)

m_radioUK   An integer variable, attached to the first radio button in the group, with its value representing the currently-selected button (0 for the first button; -1 if no button is selected)

m_staticSelection   A CString variable attached to the main label

The two non-control member variables are initialised in the dialog's constructor.

List selection

```cpp
// DialogSelect.cpp : implementation file

#include  "stdafx.h"
#include  "test.h"
#include  "DialogSelect.h"

...  // Standard conditional compilation statements omitted
///////////////////////////////////////////////////////////////////////
// CDialogSelect dialog

CDialogSelect::CDialogSelect(CWnd*  pParent  /*=NULL*/)
   : CDialog(CDialogSelect::IDD, pParent)
{
   //{{AFX_DATA_INIT(CDialogSelect)
   m_radioUK = 0;
   m_staticSelection = _T("No current selection");
   //}}AFX_DATA_INIT
}

void   CDialogSelect::DoDataExchange(CDataExchange*  pDX)
{
   CDialog::DoDataExchange(pDX);
   //{{AFX_DATA_MAP(CDialogSelect)
   DDX_Control(pDX,  IDC_EDIT_NEW_AREA,  m_editNewArea);
   DDX_Control(pDX,  IDC_COMBO_AREA,  m_comboArea);
   DDX_Radio(pDX,  IDC_RADIO_UK,  m_radioUK);
   DDX_Text(pDX,  IDC_STATIC_SELECTED,  m_staticSelection);
   //}}AFX_DATA_MAP
}

BEGIN_MESSAGE_MAP(CDialogSelect,    CDialog)
   //{{AFX_MSG_MAP(CDialogSelect)
   ON_BN_CLICKED(IDC_RADIO_UK,    OnRadioUk)
   ON_WM_SHOWWINDOW()
   ON_BN_CLICKED(IDC_RADIO_EUROPE,    OnRadioEurope)
   ON_BN_CLICKED(IDC_BUTTON_SELECT,    OnButtonSelect)
   ON_BN_CLICKED(IDC_BUTTON_ADD,    OnButtonAdd)
   //}}AFX_MSG_MAP
END_MESSAGE_MAP()

///////////////////////////////////////////////////////////////////////
// CDialogSelect message handlers
void   CDialogSelect::AddUKList()
{
   m_comboArea.ResetContent();              //Clear current contents
   m_comboArea.AddString("Scotland");
   m_comboArea.AddString("Wales");
```

Initialise radio button and label

Clear list and add new items

121

```
        m_comboArea.AddString("North");   // Add others as required
        m_comboArea.SetCurSel(0);              //Default to first item
}

void    CDialogSelect::AddEuropeList()
{
        m_comboArea.AddString("France");
        m_comboArea.AddString("Germany");
        m_comboArea.AddString("Belgium");
        m_comboArea.SetCurSel(0);              //Default to new first item
}

void CDialogSelect::OnShowWindow(BOOL bShow, UINT nStatus)
{
        CDialog::OnShowWindow(bShow,      nStatus);
        AddUKList();
}

void    CDialogSelect::OnRadioUk()
{
        AddUKList();
}

void    CDialogSelect::OnRadioEurope()
{
        AddUKList();
        AddEuropeList();
}

void    CDialogSelect::OnButtonSelect()
{
        CString   SelectedArea;
        int IndexNum = m_comboArea.GetCurSel();
        if (IndexNum != CB_ERR)
        {
            m_comboArea.GetLBText(IndexNum,      SelectedArea);
            m_staticSelection = "Current selection: " + SelectedArea;
        }
        else
        {
            m_staticSelection = "No current selection";
        }
        UpdateData(FALSE);                 //Pass data to controls
}

void    CDialogSelect::OnButtonAdd()
{
        CString   NewArea;
        m_editNewArea.GetWindowText(NewArea);
```

Add further list items

Initialise list on start-up

Respond to radio button clicks

Display new selection

```
    NewArea.TrimLeft();
    NewArea.TrimRight();

    if (NewArea != "")
    {                                          Extend the list
        m_comboArea.AddString(NewArea);
    }
}
```

There are two user-defined functions. The fist (AddUKList) starts by clearing the combo box list (using its ResetContent member function); it then refills the list (using AddString) and selects the first item in the list (with SetCurSel, which also displays the selected item in the edit part of the combo box). By default, the list is sorted alphabetically. The second user-defined function (AddEuropeList) extends the list and resets the current selection.

Five events are catered for:

● When the dialog box is first displayed, the WM_SHOWWINDOW message is despatched; this is handled by OnShowWindow, which sets up the combo box.

● There are handlers for the BN_CLICKED message for each of the radio buttons; these reset the combo box list.

● The BN_CLICKED message for the 'Select Area' button gets the current selection from the combo box (using GetCurSel, which returns the index number of the selected item). If this is a valid value (i.e. the return value is not the constant CB_ERR), the combo box's GetLBText function is used to retrieve the text for the specified index number, putting it in the variable SelectedArea. This text is copied to the member variable attached to the label. Finally, the dialog box is updated with the new variable value.

● The BN_CLICKED message for the second button defines a variable of type CString and then uses GetWindowText to load the contents of the edit box into this variable. CString has many member functions, two of which are used to trim spaces from either end of the string variable. This string (if not empty) is added to the list in the combo box.

Exercises

1 Add message handlers to the Line-drawing Features dialog box in VisDraw. When the box is displayed, the Line Thickness combo box should include options for thin, medium and thick lines; the Text Font combo box should show font sizes 8, 10 and 12 point.

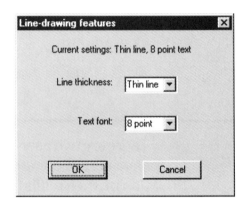

The label at the top of the dialog box should show the current line thickness and font size. Initially, the thickness should be thin and the font size 8 points.

2 Add message handlers to the VisCalc application.

If an entry is made in either of the Value boxes, the Result box should be cleared, the 'Clear All' box should be enabled and 'Copy Result to First Value' should be disabled.

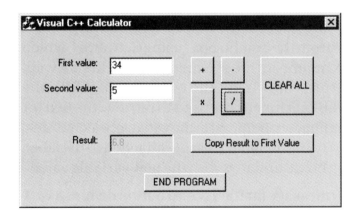

If one of the four function buttons (+ - x /) is clicked, the result of the calculation (using the two entered values) should be shown in the Result box and the 'Copy Result to First Value' box should be enabled.

The 'Clear All' button should clear the contents of the Value buttons. The 'Copy Result to First Value' button should do just that.

For solutions to these exercises, see page 178.

124

7 Documents and views

Device contexts

If you have created an SDI or MDI application, you will have a blank window on which you will want to display text or graphics. This chapter looks at ways in which you can begin to fill the white space.

Each window contains a 'logical' drawing area, where text and graphics can be drawn. Anything drawn in this area must be made to appear on the required physical device (the screen, a printer or some other output device). Windows uses a **device context** to make the link between the application and the device driver. The MFC contains a class, CDC, which includes all the functions needed for using a device context. These functions create and destroy DCs, draw lines and shapes, and draw text. Each new DC is supplied with a set of default attributes, including the background colour, drawing and painting colours, line thickness, palette, co-ordinate system and system font. There are functions for changing all of these.

When you need a device context, you must carry out the following steps:

1   Create the DC.

2   Draw the text and graphics.

3   Release the DC (an essential step, as there are only a limited number of DCs available).

Much of the time, the creation and destruction of DCs will be done for you and you need only worry about filling the window.

Co-ordinate systems

Any point on the window can be identified by a pair of (x, y) co-ordinates, the x value representing the distance across the screen from the left and the y value giving the vertical distance from top or bottom. Within the program, any point on the window is represented by a pair of **logical** co-ordinates. When the point is actually drawn, its position is translated to a pair of **physical** co-ordinates, giving its actual position on the window (which may vary, depending on the type of monitor or printer being used).

The way in which the translation is carried out is determined by the **mapping mode**. The default is MM_TEXT (in which each logical unit represents one pixel) but you can change this to various other modes:

MM_HIENGLISH	(0.001 inch)
MM_LOENGLISH	(0.01 inch)
MM_TWIPS	(1/1440 inch)
MM_HIMETRIC	(0.01 mm)
MM_LOMETRIC	(0.1mm)
MM_ISOTROPIC	(User-defined)
MM_ANISOTROPIC	(User-defined)

The first five of these put the Y-axis origin at the bottom of the window.

For the MM_ANISOTROPIC mode, the relationship between logical and physical units is not necessarily the same for x and y axes; for all other modes, a logical unit represents the same physical unit horizontally and vertically.

The CPoint class

Positions on the screen can be specified by two separate integers, representing the x and y values. Alternatively, you can use a CPoint object which holds an (x, y) pair. The CPoint structure contains the separate x and y values, which can be used or changed explicitly. For example:

```
CPoint  StartPos;
StartPos.x = 50;
StartPos.y = 100;
```

This code creates a variable StartPos of type CPoint and gives it an initial value of (50,100): that is, StartPos is now indicating a point 50 pixels from the left-hand side of the screen and 100 points down (assuming the mapping mode is still MM_TEXT).

Displaying text

To demonstrate the drawing of text on the screen, the Notebook program will display a string when the left mouse button is clicked, with the top-left corner of the text being at the pointer position.

The program must remember the pointer position when the button is clicked, so a global variable is needed. All the work for this demonstration will be done in the view class (CNotebookView). In ClassView, right-click on CNotebookView and select Add Member Variable. The Variable Type should be CPoint (so that the variable can store a pair of co-ordinates) and the Variable Declaration should be TextPos; the Access type should be Protected.

The pointer position must be captured when the left mouse button is clicked. In the Message Maps tab of ClassWizard, select CNotebookView as the Object ID and WM_LBUTTONDOWN as the message. Click on Add Function, then on Edit Code. You are provided with a default message handler that includes a call to the base class's equivalent function.

The function has two parameters passed to it:

- The **nFlags** variable, of type UINT (unsigned integer), holds a value indicating whether the **[Ctrl]** or **[Shift]** keys or another mouse button are being pressed.

- The **point** variable, of type CPoint, holds the co-ordinates of the mouse pointer when the button was pressed.

It is the 'point' value that is of interest in this case.

Take note

For each mouse button, there are messages for when the button is pressed down, released or double-clicked. There is no message for a click, so you need to choose between the button down and button up messages, depending on when you want the action to happen.

Two new lines should be added to the function, so that it looks like this:

```
void    CNotebookView::OnLButtonDown(UINT    nFlags,
                                                CPoint  point)
{
    TextPos = point;
    Invalidate();
    CView::OnLButtonDown(nFlags,    point);
}
```

The first line of the function code copies the current co-ordinates into the global variable, TextPos. The second line calls the Invalidate function, which forces Windows to repaint the window. The third line calls the equivalent function of the base class, to carry out any other necessary work.

As part of the repainting process, the OnDraw function is called. A new statement should be added to the end of the default function:

```
void    CNotebookView::OnDraw(CDC*    pDC)
{
    CNotebookDoc*  pDoc = GetDocument();
    ASSERT_VALID(pDoc);
    pDC->TextOut(TextPos.x,  TextPos.y,  "Here  we  are!");
}
```

The function has as its parameter a pointer to a CDC object, pDC. The object pointed to by pDC contains the device context functions, amongst which is **TextOut**, a function that displays a given piece of text at a specified (x, y) position. In this case, the position is held in the TextPos variable and can therefore be broken down into its x and y components. The text is a constant here.

You can now compile and run the program. Each time you click on the window, the piece of text will appear at the pointer position. The positions are not being stored, so the text disappears from its old position each time the window is repainted.

Drawing lines

The program will now be extended so that a line is drawn on the window when the mouse is dragged with the right button pressed. This time, the co-ordinates of each new line will be stored so that the effect is cumulative. It is here that the split between the document and view classes becomes apparent:

- The document class stores the data used for the display and is responsible for saving and retrieving the data.

- The view class controls the display of the data.

Each of these classes has member functions suited to its own responsibilities.

Storing the data

The data will be stored by the document class, and three variables are needed: two arrays of points to hold the start and end of each line, and a variable to show how many points have been stored so far. These variables are added by right-clicking on CNoteBookDoc in the ClassView and selecting Add Member Variable.

The information to be entered is as follows:

	Variable 1	*Variable 2*	*Variable 3*
Variable Type	CPoint	CPoint	UINT
Variable Declaration	LineStart[20]	LineEnd[20]	LineIndex
Access	Public	Public	Public

Note that the declaration must include the array dimensions (just as it would if the declaration were being entered manually). It is also important that these variables are declared as **public** variables, as they will have to be accessed from the view class. You can see the effect of adding these variables by inspecting the NotebookDoc.h file.

Document header file

```
// NotebookDoc.h : interface of the CNotebookDoc class
//
/////////////////////////////////////////////////////////////////

#if      !defined(AFX_NOTEBOOKDOC_H__C62725BF_..._INCLUDED_)
#define      AFX_NOTEBOOKDOC_H__C62725BF_..._INCLUDED_

#if _MSC_VER >= 1000
#pragma once
#endif // _MSC_VER >= 1000

class CNotebookDoc : public CDocument
{
protected: // create from serialization only
    CNotebookDoc();
    DECLARE_DYNCREATE(CNotebookDoc)

// Attributes
public:

// Operations
public:

// Overrides
    // ClassWizard generated virtual function overrides
    //{{AFX_VIRTUAL(CNotebookDoc)
    public:
    virtual  BOOL  OnNewDocument();
    virtual void Serialize(CArchive& ar);
    //}}AFX_VIRTUAL

// Implementation
public:
    UINT  LineIndex;
    CPoint  LineEnd[20];
    CPoint  LineStart[20];
    virtual  ~CNotebookDoc();
#ifdef _DEBUG
    virtual void AssertValid() const;
    virtual void Dump(CDumpContext& dc) const;
#endif

protected:

// Generated message map functions
protected:
    //{{AFX_MSG(CNotebookDoc)
```

Member function overrides

Member variables

131

```
          // NOTE - the ClassWizard will add and remove here.
          //    DO NOT EDIT what you see in these blocks of code !
      //}}AFX_MSG
      DECLARE_MESSAGE_MAP()
};

//////////////////////////////////////////////////////////////////

//{{AFX_INSERT_LOCATION}}
// Microsoft Developer Studio will insert additional declarations
// immediately before the previous line.

#endif //
!defined(AFX_NOTEBOOKDOC_H__C62725BF_..._INCLUDED_)
```

This file has many of the components of the other C++ header files described earlier. Two functions (which replace those defined in the base class) are declared in the Overrides section:

● **OnNewDocument**, which performs any necessary initialisation when the document is created

● **Serialize**, which handles the reading and writing of files

The Implementation section contains the new variable definitions.

Initialising the variables

The final change to make to the document class is to initialise the LineIndex variable. This is done by adding a single line to the OnNewDocument function in the source file (NotebookDoc.cpp):

```
LineIndex = 0;
```

There is little else that is new in the source file (shown below).

Note that, in both listings, some standard statements have been abbreviated to save space.

Document source file

```
// NotebookDoc.cpp : implementation of CNotebookDoc class
//

#include   "stdafx.h"
#include   "Notebook.h"
#include   "NotebookDoc.h"

#ifdef  _DEBUG
#define  new  DEBUG_NEW
#undef  THIS_FILE
static  char  THIS_FILE[]  =  __FILE__;
#endif
/////////////////////////////////////////////////////////////////////
//  CNotebookDoc

IMPLEMENT_DYNCREATE(CNotebookDoc,        CDocument)

BEGIN_MESSAGE_MAP(CNotebookDoc,        CDocument)
   //{{AFX_MSG_MAP(CNotebookDoc)
      // NOTE - the ClassWizard will add and remove macros here.
      //     DO NOT EDIT what you see in these blocks of code!
   //}}AFX_MSG_MAP
END_MESSAGE_MAP()

/////////////////////////////////////////////////////////////////////
//  CNotebookDoc   construction/destruction

CNotebookDoc::CNotebookDoc()
{
   // TODO: add one-time construction code here
}

CNotebookDoc::~CNotebookDoc()
{
}

BOOL     CNotebookDoc::OnNewDocument()
{
   if   (!CDocument::OnNewDocument())
      return  FALSE;

   LineIndex = 0;

   // TODO: add reinitialization code here
   // (SDI documents will reuse this document)
   return  TRUE;
}
```

Initialisation of member variable

133

```
/////////////////////////////////////////////////////////////////////////
// CNotebookDoc  serialization

void   CNotebookDoc::Serialize(CArchive&   ar)
{
    if (ar.IsStoring())
    {
        // TODO:  add  storing  code  here
    }
    else
    {
        // TODO:  add  loading  code  here
    }
}

/////////////////////////////////////////////////////////////////////////
// CNotebookDoc  diagnostics

#ifdef  _DEBUG
void   CNotebookDoc::AssertValid()   const
{
    CDocument::AssertValid();
}

void   CNotebookDoc::Dump(CDumpContext&   dc)   const
{
    CDocument::Dump(dc);
}
#endif  //_DEBUG

/////////////////////////////////////////////////////////////////////////
// CNotebookDoc  commands
```

Take note

When this file was created, three of the functions were set up ready for you to add code: the constructor (CNotebookDoc), OnNewDocument (for initialisation) and Serialize (for reading and writing data). You can add to these functions at any time.

Responding to right-clicks

All that remains is to draw a line when the mouse is dragged with the right-hand mouse button pressed. Two events must be trapped: WM_RBUTTONDOWN and WM_RBUTTONUP. Using ClassWizard, select the CNotebookView class and add the OnRButtonDown and OnRButtonUp message handlers. Then add the code needed to draw the lines. The relevant parts of the header and source files are shown below. The remaining parts are similar to those of other classes.

View header file

```
// NotebookView.h : interface of the CNotebookView class
...
class CNotebookView : public CView
{
...
// Attributes
public:
    CNotebookDoc*    GetDocument();
// Overrides
    // ClassWizard generated virtual function overrides
    //{{AFX_VIRTUAL(CNotebookView)
    public:
    virtual void OnDraw(CDC* pDC);   // overridden to draw this view
    virtual  BOOL  PreCreateWindow(CREATESTRUCT&  cs);
    protected:
    virtual  BOOL OnPreparePrinting(CPrintInfo* pInfo);
    virtual  void OnBeginPrinting(CDC* pDC, CPrintInfo* pInfo);
    virtual  void OnEndPrinting(CDC* pDC, CPrintInfo* pInfo);
    //}}AFX_VIRTUAL
// Implementation
...
// Generated message map functions
protected:
    BOOL   CreatingLine;
    CPoint  TextPos;
    //{{AFX_MSG(CNotebookView)
    afx_msg void OnRButtonDown(UINT nFlags, CPoint point);
    afx_msg void OnRButtonUp(UINT nFlags, CPoint point);
    afx_msg void OnLButtonDown(UINT nFlags, CPoint point);
    //}}AFX_MSG
    DECLARE_MESSAGE_MAP()
};
...
```

New message handlers

135

```
// NotebookView.cpp : implementation of the CNotebookView class

#include   "stdafx.h"
#include   "Notebook.h"
#include   "NotebookDoc.h"
#include   "NotebookView.h"
...
/////////////////////////////////////////////////////////////////////////////
//   CNotebookView
IMPLEMENT_DYNCREATE(CNotebookView,      CView)

BEGIN_MESSAGE_MAP(CNotebookView,      CView)
   //{{AFX_MSG_MAP(CNotebookView)
   ON_WM_RBUTTONDOWN()
   ON_WM_RBUTTONUP()
   ON_WM_LBUTTONDOWN()
   //}}AFX_MSG_MAP
   // Standard printing commands
   ON_COMMAND(ID_FILE_PRINT,       CView::OnFilePrint)
   ON_COMMAND(ID_FILE_PRINT_DIRECT,       CView::OnFilePrint)
   ON_COMMAND(ID_FILE_PRINT_PREVIEW,
CView::OnFilePrintPreview)
END_MESSAGE_MAP()


/////////////////////////////////////////////////////////////////////////////
//   CNotebookView   construction/destruction

CNotebookView::CNotebookView()
{
   // TODO: add construction code here
}


CNotebookView::~CNotebookView()
{
}


BOOL   CNotebookView::PreCreateWindow(CREATESTRUCT&    cs)
{
   // TODO: Modify the Window class or styles here by modifying
   //   the CREATESTRUCT cs
   return    CView::PreCreateWindow(cs);
}


/////////////////////////////////////////////////////////////////////////////
// CNotebookView   drawing
void   CNotebookView::OnDraw(CDC*   pDC)
{
```

Revised   message   map

136

```
        CNotebookDoc* pDoc = GetDocument();
        ASSERT_VALID(pDoc);

        pDC->TextOut(TextPos.x, TextPos.y, "Here we are!");
        UINT x1, y1, x2, y2;
        UINT MaxIndex;
        MaxIndex = pDoc->LineIndex;
        for (UINT i = 0; i < MaxIndex; ++i)
        {
            x1 = pDoc->LineStart[i].x;
            y1 = pDoc->LineStart[i].y;
            x2 = pDoc->LineEnd[i].x;
            y2 = pDoc->LineEnd[i].y;
            pDC->MoveTo(x1, y1);
            pDC->LineTo(x2, y2);
        }
    }


    /////////////////////////////////////////////////////////////////
    // CNotebookView printing

    BOOL   CNotebookView::OnPreparePrinting(CPrintInfo*   pInfo)
    {
        // default preparation
        return  DoPreparePrinting(pInfo);
    }

    void   CNotebookView::OnBeginPrinting(CDC*   /*pDC*/,
                                               CPrintInfo*   /*pInfo*/)
    {
        // TODO: add extra initialization before printing
    }

    void   CNotebookView::OnEndPrinting(CDC*   /*pDC*/,
                                             CPrintInfo*   /*pInfo*/)
    {
        // TODO: add cleanup after printing
    }

    /////////////////////////////////////////////////////////////////
    // CNotebookView diagnostics

    #ifdef _DEBUG
    void  CNotebookView::AssertValid()  const
    {
        CView::AssertValid();
    }
```

Display text

Display lines

```
void  CNotebookView::Dump(CDumpContext&  dc)  const
{
    CView::Dump(dc);
}

CNotebookDoc*  CNotebookView::GetDocument()  //  non-debug
version  is  inline
{
    ASSERT(m_pDocument->IsKindOf(RUNTIME_CLASS(CNotebookDoc)));
    return    (CNotebookDoc*)m_pDocument;
}
#endif  //_DEBUG

//////////////////////////////////////////////////////////////////////////
//  CNotebookView  message  handlers

void  CNotebookView::OnLButtonDown(UINT  nFlags,  CPoint  point)
{
    TextPos = point;
    Invalidate();

    CView::OnLButtonDown(nFlags,    point);
}

void  CNotebookView::OnRButtonDown(UINT  nFlags,  CPoint  point)
{
    CNotebookDoc*  pDoc  =  GetDocument();
    if (pDoc->LineIndex >= 20)
        return;

    pDoc->LineStart[pDoc->LineIndex]  =  point;
    pDoc->SetModifiedFlag();
    Invalidate();
    CView::OnRButtonDown(nFlags,    point);
}

void  CNotebookView::OnRButtonUp(UINT  nFlags,  CPoint  point)
{
    CNotebookDoc*  pDoc  =  GetDocument();
    if (pDoc->LineIndex >= 20)
        return;

    pDoc->LineEnd[pDoc->LineIndex]  =  point;
    pDoc->LineIndex++;
    pDoc->SetModifiedFlag();
    Invalidate();
    CView::OnRButtonUp(nFlags,    point);
}
```

Store text position

Store line start

Store line end

138

The OnRButtonDown function begins with the line:

```
CNotebookDoc*  pDoc  =  GetDocument();
```

GetDocument returns a pointer (pDoc) to the CNotebookDoc object that is associated with the view. This allows the function to call the member functions from the document and access its public variables.

The next statement checks that the limit on the arrays has not been reached. If it hasn't, the current pointer positions (passed to the function as a parameter, point) is stored in the next slot in the LineStart array. (If you want to add more than 20 lines, amend the two array declarations in the document header and the two limit checks in this file.)

The SetModifiedFlag function (from the document class) marks the fact that the data for that document has been changed. The effect is that when you leave the program will be asked if you want to save the data.

The Invalidate function forces Window to redraw the window. The function ends with a call to the equivalent function from the base class.

OnRButtonUp performs similar operations, this time storing the current position in the LineEnd array and also incrementing the LineIndex Value.

The other changes are to OnDraw, which is called whenever the window is redrawn. This function now contains a loop that draws each line. The start and end points are broken down into their separate x and y co-ordinates, which can then be used in the device context's MoveTo and LineTo functions. MoveTo moves the drawing position to the first point; LineTo draws a line from there to the second point.

You can now compile and run this program. It should allow you to draw up to 20 lines on the screen using the right-hand mouse button, or move a piece of text with the left button.

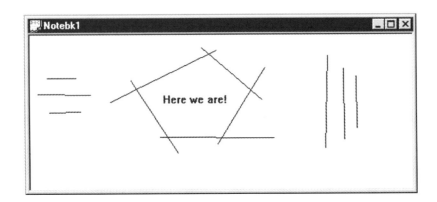

Other shapes

The CDC class has a large number of drawing functions, like MoveTo and LineTo. These can be used to draw different shapes on the screen. The drawing functions include:

- **Rectangle**, which draws a rectangle between two points (and therefore takes four co-ordinates as its parameters)

- **RoundRect**, which draws a rectangle with rounded corners

- **Pie**, which draws a wedge

- **Ellipse**, which draws an ellipse within a specified rectangle (and produces a circle if the two points given mark out a square)

- **Arc**, which draws an arc from an ellipse (or circle)

There are also functions for drawing polygons and lines with many segments.

You can try any of these by replacing the LineTo statement in the OnDraw function. For example, to draw rectangles instead of straight lines, replace the LineTo statement with the following:

```
pDC->Rectangle(x1, y1, x2, y2);
```

Now when you drag the mouse pointer you will draw a series of boxes on the screen.

Take note

You can change the colour, size and fill pattern of lines and shapes — see page 145.

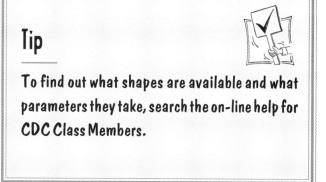

Tip

To find out what shapes are available and what parameters they take, search the on-line help for CDC Class Members.

Enhanced ·line drawing

The program, as it stands, allows you to draw a number of lines but the lines only become visible when they have been finished. To allow you to see the lines as they are being drawn, you need to respond to the WM_MOUSEMOVE message, which is despatched every time the mouse moves.

The revised functions are shown below. There is a new protected member variable, of type BOOL, called CreatingLine. When TRUE, this indicates that a line is being drawn (i.e. the right-hand mouse button is down). The CreatingLine flag is initialised in PreCreateWindow, a function that is called when the view is first created. The flag is then set to TRUE when the right-hand button is pressed and cleared when the button is released.

An extra message handler, OnMouseMove, forces the window to be redrawn whenever the mouse moves; OnDraw has been amended so that a new line is drawn if CreatingLine is TRUE. The result is that you can see the line you have created, although it does tend to create a flicker effect on the window while the line is being drawn.

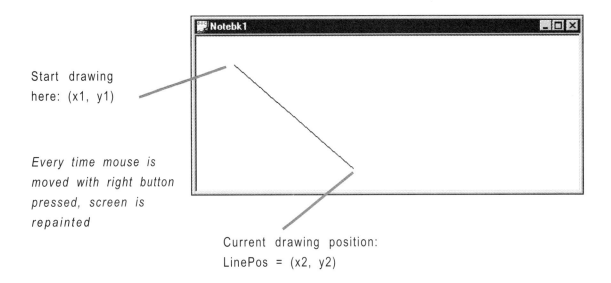

Start drawing here: (x1, y1)

Every time mouse is moved with right button pressed, screen is repainted

Current drawing position: LinePos = (x2, y2)

Enhanced drawing

```
BOOL    CNotebookView::PreCreateWindow(CREATESTRUCT&    cs)
{
    CreatingLine = FALSE;

    return    CView::PreCreateWindow(cs);
}

void   CNotebookView::OnDraw(CDC*   pDC)
{
    CNotebookDoc* pDoc = GetDocument();
    ASSERT_VALID(pDoc);

    UINT x1, y1, x2, y2;

    UINT  MaxIndex;
    MaxIndex  =  pDoc->LineIndex;

    pDC->TextOut(TextPos.x,  TextPos.y,  "Here  we  are!");

    for (UINT i = 0; i < MaxIndex; ++i)
    {
        x1  =  pDoc->LineStart[i].x;
        y1  =  pDoc->LineStart[i].y;
        x2  =  pDoc->LineEnd[i].x;
        y2  =  pDoc->LineEnd[i].y;

        pDC->MoveTo(x1,    y1);
        pDC->LineTo(x2,    y2);
    }

    if  (CreatingLine)
    {
        x1  =  pDoc->LineStart[MaxIndex].x;
        y1  =  pDoc->LineStart[MaxIndex].y;
        x2 = LinePos.x;
        y2 = LinePos.y;

        pDC->MoveTo(x1,    y1);
        pDC->LineTo(x2,    y2);
    }
}

void  CNotebookView::OnRButtonDown(UINT  nFlags,  CPoint  point)
{
    CNotebookDoc*  pDoc  =  GetDocument();
```

Initialise flag (indicating no line being drawn at present)

Draw the line that is currently being created

```
    if (pDoc->LineIndex >= 20)
        return;

    pDoc->LineStart[pDoc->LineIndex]  =  point;
    CreatingLine  =  TRUE;

    pDoc->SetModifiedFlag();
    Invalidate();

    CView::OnRButtonDown(nFlags,    point);
}

void  CNotebookView::OnRButtonUp(UINT  nFlags,  CPoint  point)
{
    CNotebookDoc*  pDoc  =  GetDocument();

    if (pDoc->LineIndex >= 20)
        return;

    pDoc->LineEnd[pDoc->LineIndex]  =  point;
    pDoc->LineIndex++;

    CreatingLine  =  FALSE;

    pDoc->SetModifiedFlag();
    Invalidate();

    CView::OnRButtonUp(nFlags,    point);
}

void  CNotebookView::OnMouseMove(UINT  nFlags,  CPoint  point)
{
    LinePos = point;

    if  (CreatingLine)
    {
        Invalidate();
    }

    CView::OnMouseMove(nFlags,    point);
}
```

Set flag (to indicate that a line is being drawn now)

Clear flag (line has been finished)

Redraw window whenever the mouse is moved

144

Device context attributes

The example above draws lines and text on the surface of the window, using the defaults that are supplied with the device context when it is created. However, all of these defaults can be changed; some of the more useful DC attributes are described here.

The pen

Whenever you draw a line or shape on the window, it is drawn with a particular style, thickness and colour. By default, the device context draws a solid, thin, black line but any of these attributes can be altered.

The line-drawing attributes are stored in a **pen** object, derived from the class CPen. To change any aspect of the pen you must create a new pen, specifying the required style, thickness and colour. The statement takes the form:

```
CPen NewPen(style, thickness, colour);
```

This creates a pen object called NewPen. The *style* determines whether the line is solid or broken and can be any of the following:

PS_SOLID	PS_DASH	PS_DOT
PS_DASHDOT	PS_DASHDOTDOT	
PS_NULL	PS_INSIDEFRAME	

You can also include a value that specifies the style for the ends of the line (such as PS_ENDCAP_ROUND or PS_ENDCAP_SQUARE) and the way in which lines are joined (e.g. PS_JOIN_BEVEL). The components of the style are combined with the OR (|) operator. For example, the style for a solid line with square ends would be:

```
PS_SOLID | PS_ENDCAP_SQUARE
```

The *thickness* is an integer, with the thinnest possible line being one pixel wide (even though it has a thickness of 0).

The *colour* is most easily defined using the RGB function, which takes three parameters:

```
RGB(red, green, blue)
```

145

Each parameter can take a value in the range 0 to 255. For example, RGB(0,0,0) represents black, RGB(255,255,255) is white and RGB(255, 0, 0) gives you pure red.

Having created the pen, you must pass it to the device context using the SelectObject function. The following two statements will increase the thickness of the line and change its colour to blue:

```
CPen NewPen(PS_SOLID, 2, RGB(0, 0, 255));
pDC->SelectObject(&NewPen);
```

The brush

When you draw a shape that encloses a part of the window (such as a rectangle or ellipse), the device context determines the colour and pattern used to fill the shape. These attributes are stored in a **brush** object, derived from the class CBrush. As for the pen, you can create a new brush with a statement in the form:

```
CBrush NewBrush(pattern, colour);
```

The *pattern* can be any of the following:

HS_BDIAGONAL	HS_CROSS	HS_DIAGCROSS
HS_FDIAGONAL	HS_HORIZONTAL	HS_VERTICAL

If omitted, the shape is filled with solid colour. The colour is specified in the same way as for CPen and the brush is passed to the device context using the same SelectObject function. For example:

```
CBrush NewBrush(RGB(0, 128, 128));
pDC->SelectObject(&NewBrush);
```

Any closed shapes will now be filled with solid purple.

Fonts

The font for text drawn on the screen can also be changed. This is a somewhat more complex task. The following function demonstrates how the font can be altered.

```
void   CNotebookView::SetUpFont(CDC*   pDC)
{
    LOGFONT   NewFont;

    NewFont.lfHeight  =  8;
    NewFont.lfWidth  =  0;
    NewFont.lfEscapement  =  0;
    NewFont.lfOrientation  =  0;
    NewFont.lfWeight  =  0;
    NewFont.lfItalic  =  0;
    NewFont.lfUnderline  =  0;
    NewFont.lfStrikeOut  =  0;
    NewFont.lfCharSet  =  ANSI_CHARSET;
    NewFont.lfOutPrecision  =  OUT_DEFAULT_PRECIS;
    NewFont.lfClipPrecision  =  CLIP_DEFAULT_PRECIS;
    NewFont.lfQuality  =  DEFAULT_QUALITY;
    NewFont.lfPitchAndFamily  =  DEFAULT_PITCH  |  FF_MODERN;
    strcpy(NewFont.lfFaceName,   "Arial");

    CFont  FontObj;
    FontObj.CreateFontIndirect(&NewFont);
    pDC->SelectObject(&FontObj);
}
```

The function defines a variable with the LOGFONT structure, which holds the definition of a font. The various components of the structure are then set to default values.

Following on from this, a CFont object is created and its CreateIndirectFont function is called, with the LOGFONT structure as a parameter. The function sets up a font that matches as closely as possible the attributes specified in the structure (the end effect will depend on the fonts installed on the PC). Finally, the CFont object is passed to the device context, using the same SelectObject function as before.

To implement this font you need only call the function with a statement such as:

```
SetUpFont(pDC);
```

You can, of course, change any of the values stored in the LOGFONT structure. For a full explanation of the font components, search the on-line help for 'LOGFONT structure'.

Serialisation

The data created on a window is written away to file through a process called **Serialisation**. The document class includes a **Serialize** member function, which has the responsibility for writing and reading data. When the application is created, the Serialize function is added, with a basic structure set up. This function is called by the standard Open, Save and Save As options in the application's File menu. It is also invoked if the user saves the data on closing the window.

The function uses a CArchive object, which saves data in binary form. An archive is the equivalent of a standard C input/output stream, in that it is associated with a file and transfers buffered input and output to and from the file. The details of how all this is achieved is hidden from you; at its simplest, all you need to do is amend the Serialize function to write and read data.

The Serialize function contains an 'if' statement that tests the result of the archive's IsStoring function. This function returns a Boolean value: TRUE if the archive is being used for storing data, FALSE if data is being loaded. The archive uses a << operator for writing data to the archive and >> for reading it back. For example, the following statement writes an item of *data* to the archive:

```
ar << data;
```

The *data* can be a number or a piece of text. Similarly, this statement retrieves the data:

```
ar >> data;
```

In the example below, the Serialize function for the sample application has been modified to allow the line co-ordinates to be written to file. The first part of the function writes away the components of the line start and end co-ordinates, finally storing a value of -1 to indicate the end of the data.

The second part of the function reads back the data until the -1 is encountered. The LineIndex variable is updated so that it holds the number of lines drawn. Data can therefore be read in and new lines added up to the maximum specified by the array.

You don't need to worry about the filename here. The association between the archive and a file is handled by the Open and Save dialogs. When you select the File | Open or File | Save As commands you are asked to choose a file, of the type specified when the application was created. The File | Save command rewrites the file associated with the current window. Simple file handling is therefore a relatively straightforward process under Visual C++.

Serialisation

```
// CNotebookDoc  serialization

void  CNotebookDoc::Serialize(CArchive&  ar)
{
    if (ar.IsStoring())                    //storing data
    {
        for (UINT i = 0; i < LineIndex; ++i)
        {
            ar << LineStart[i].x;
            ar << LineStart[i].y;
            ar << LineEnd[i].x;
            ar << LineEnd[i].y;
        }
        ar << -1;
    }
    else                    //loading data
    {
        int x1 = 0;
        LineIndex = 0;
        while (x1 != -1)
        {
            ar >> x1;
            if (x1 != -1)
            {
                LineStart[LineIndex].x = x1;
                ar >> LineStart[LineIndex].y;
                ar >> LineEnd[LineIndex].x;
                ar >> LineEnd[LineIndex].y;
                LineIndex++;
            }
        }
    }
}
```

Write data to file

Read data from file

149

Exercises

1 Add functions to the VisDraw application to allow it to display a small blue square when the left-hand mouse button is clicked and a small red circle when the right-hand button is clicked. Allow for up to 100 such objects.

2 Add a function to allow text to be typed to the right of each new symbol. (Use the WM_KEYDOWN function.)

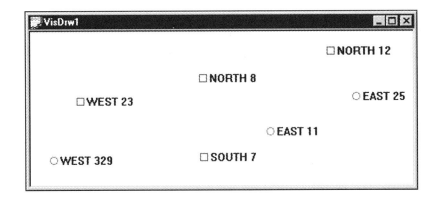

3 Implement the function to save and retrieve the information needed to create the display (symbols and text).

For solutions to these exercises, see page 183.

8 Programming options

Debugging

This chapter considers some of the extra options that are available when programming in C++. One of the most important of these is the ability to debug the program: to trace through it, line by line, as it is executed and to inspect the values of variables.

The simplest way to start debugging is with the Build | Start Debug | Go option – or just press **[F5]**. The program starts running in the usual way but the Debug toolbar should appear behind it.

Stop
Debugging   Break execution   Advanced   options

Most of the options are greyed out but two are applicable at this stage:

- **Stop Debugging**, which closes down the program

- **Break Execution**, which temporarily halts the program so that you can step through it a line at a time or inspect variable values.

The options that are available when you have broken into a program are described below.

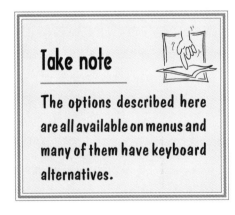

Take note

The options described here are all available on menus and many of them have keyboard alternatives.

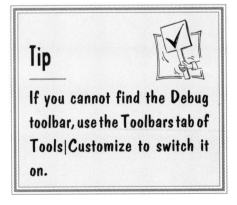

Tip

If you cannot find the Debug toolbar, use the Toolbars tab of Tools|Customize to switch it on.

Breakpoints

You can force Visual C++ to halt execution at a particular point in the program by setting a breakpoint. Before running the program, put the cursor on the required line, right-click and select Insert/Remove Breakpoint. A brown circle is displayed on the left of the line. When the program is run, it will halt at this point, before the line is executed.

Having interrupted the program in this way, you can inspect the contents of variables, step through the code a line at a time, make minor changes to the code, or continue execution.

You can set several breakpoints at once; the program halts each time a breakpoint is encountered. A breakpoint is cancelled by right-clicking on the line and selecting Remove Breakpoint. Alternatively, the breakpoint can be suspended by selecting Disable Breakpoint.

Take note

You can also set conditional breakpoints, where the break only occurs when an expression satisfies a particular condition. Use Edit|Breakpoints.

Single-stepping

When a program halts because of a break or a breakpoint, the line that is about to be executed is indicated by a yellow arrow on the left. Further options become available on the Debug toolbar. You can now run the program a line at a time using the following options:

● Click on **Step Into** to execute the line; if the line contains a procedure or a function call, the procedure or function is displayed and you can continue to step through it a line at a time. This is called **single-stepping**.

● Click on **Step Over** to execute the line, including any procedure or function call; the next line in the current procedure is then highlighted.

● Click on **Step Out** to execute to the end of the current function.

● Move the cursor to some other point in the program and click on **Run to Cursor**; execution continues until this point is reached.

- If you lose your place in the code, click on **Show Next Statement** to find the yellow arrow again.

When you have finished single-stepping, you can continue running with **[F5]** or stop with **[Shift-F5]**.

Watching variables

Having broken into a program, you can inspect the values of any variables or expressions. If you put the cursor on a variable name in the code, the current value pops up below the name.

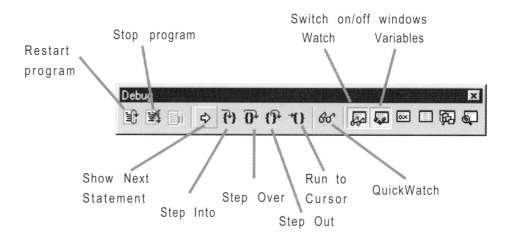

You can also see how the value changes as the program progresses. Highlight a variable name or expression in the code; then click on the QuickWatch button on the Debug toolbar. The QuickWatch window is displayed, showing the expression and its current value. Click on AddWatch to add the expression to the Watch window. Now, as you single-step through the program, you will be able to see how the values of variables are affected by the code, making it much easier to identify the causes of problems. The Variables window shows the current values of all relevant variables.

Expression
to watch

Current value of
expression

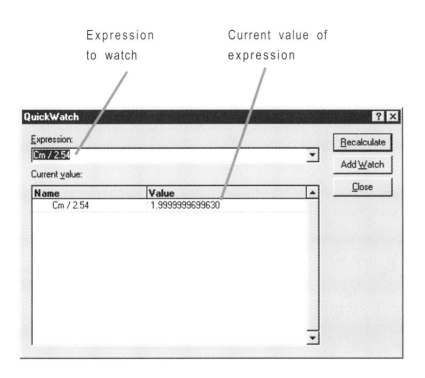

Current value of
expression or
variable

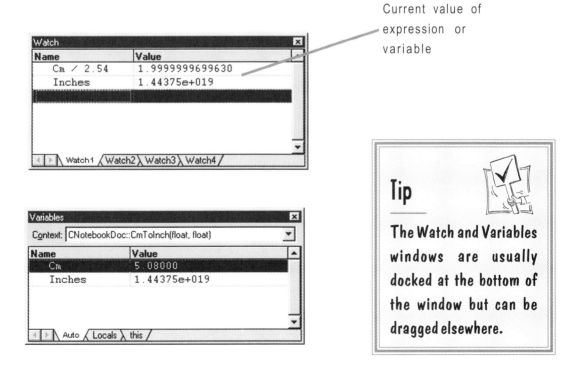

Tip

The Watch and Variables
windows are usually
docked at the bottom of
the window but can be
dragged elsewhere.

Menus

Menus at the top of the windows are added to the application as resources. To view or change a menu, select ResourceView in the Project Workspace window and expand the Menu folder. AppWizard has given you two sets of menus to start with:

IDR_MAINFRAME   A reduced menu set (containing File, View and Help menus), which appears when all secondary windows are closed

IDR_*name*TYPE   A full menu set, displayed when a secondary window is open

You can view either of these menus by double-clicking on them. The Menu Editor is displayed, giving you a number of options:

● To add a new menu, double-click on the grey box to the right of Help, then fill in the properties (see below).

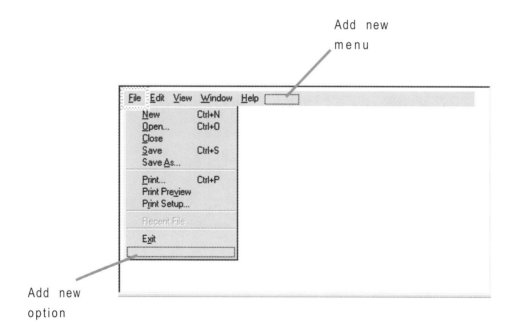

Add new menu

Add new option

● To add an option to a menu, click on the menu name, double-click on the blank item at the bottom of the list and then fill in the properties.

- To change the order of the menus, drag a menu to a new position on the top line.

- To change the order of the options in a menu, drag an option up or down.

- To promote an option to a menu or vice versa, or to move an option to a different menu, drag it to its new position, using the guide bars to see where it will end up.

- To delete an option or menu, click on it and then press **[Del]**.

Menu properties

Each menu has two important properties:

- The **Caption** is the word or phrase that will appear on the menu bar. Include an & in front of a character for that to become the menu's access key.

- The **Grayed** property, if set, greys out the menu name and makes it inactive.

The other properties can usually be left as they are.

Menu properties

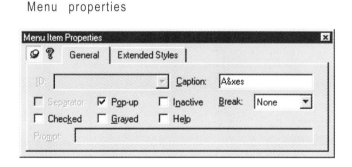

Menu option properties

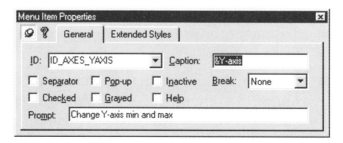

For menu options, the essential properties are these:

● The **ID** uniquely identifies the option within the set of menus. This will be generated by the system.

● The **Caption** is the name that will appear on the menu. Use & to add an access key. By convention, the Caption should end with three dots if the menu item leads to a dialog box.

● The **Separator** property, if set, inserts a separator bar in the menu. (All other properties become irrelevant.)

● The **Checked** property places a tick next to the item.

● The **Grayed** property makes the option temporarily inactive.

● The **Pop-up** property, if set, allows you to create a sub-menu for the option.

● The **Prompt** is the piece of text that is displayed on the status line when the option is highlighted.

Tip

You can view or change the prompts for all menus using the String Table — see page 161.

Take note

The ID only appears in the Properties box when you re-enter the box.

Accelerators

You can attach an accelerator to any option; this is a key combination that activates the menu without the need to open up the menu. The procedure is as follows:

1   In ResourceView, open the Accelerator folder and double-click on IDR_MAINFRAME. (Although this is the same name as the reduced menu, the accelerator table actually relates to the application as a whole.)

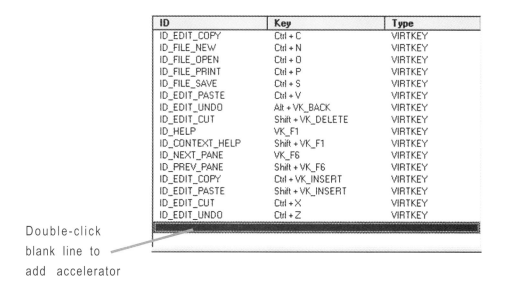

ID	Key	Type
ID_EDIT_COPY	Ctrl + C	VIRTKEY
ID_FILE_NEW	Ctrl + N	VIRTKEY
ID_FILE_OPEN	Ctrl + O	VIRTKEY
ID_FILE_PRINT	Ctrl + P	VIRTKEY
ID_FILE_SAVE	Ctrl + S	VIRTKEY
ID_EDIT_PASTE	Ctrl + V	VIRTKEY
ID_EDIT_UNDO	Alt + VK_BACK	VIRTKEY
ID_EDIT_CUT	Shift + VK_DELETE	VIRTKEY
ID_HELP	VK_F1	VIRTKEY
ID_CONTEXT_HELP	Shift + VK_F1	VIRTKEY
ID_NEXT_PANE	VK_F6	VIRTKEY
ID_PREV_PANE	Shift + VK_F6	VIRTKEY
ID_EDIT_COPY	Ctrl + VK_INSERT	VIRTKEY
ID_EDIT_PASTE	Shift + VK_INSERT	VIRTKEY
ID_EDIT_CUT	Ctrl + X	VIRTKEY
ID_EDIT_UNDO	Ctrl + Z	VIRTKEY

Double-click blank line to add accelerator

2   Double-click on the blank line at the bottom of the list. The Properties box is displayed.

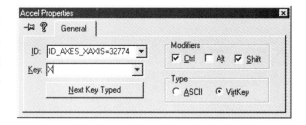

3.   Select the ID of the menu option from the drop-down list.

159

Take note

A virtual key is an ID representing one of the special keys: e.g. VK_DELETE for the [Del] key.

4. Press the Next Key Typed button and then press the required key combination. (Alternatively, type the letter or choose a 'virtual' key from the drop-down list, and select the modifiers that are to be applied to the key.)

5. Click on another entry in the table to accept the changes. The new accelerator is placed in the table in key order.

Menu events

The last stage of adding a menu option is to provide a message handler.

1. Open ClassWizard and select the appropriate class (either the document class or the view class, depending on whether the menu option will be changing data or affecting the operation of the program).

2. Choose the Object ID for the menu option (e.g. ID_AXES_YAXIS).

3. Click on the COMMAND message.

4. Click on Add Function and accept the default function name (e.g. OnAxesYaxis).

5. Click on Edit Code to add the message handler instructions.

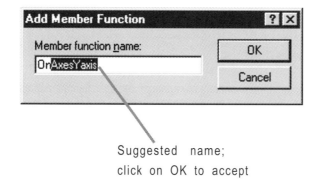

Suggested name;
click on OK to accept

Take note

If there is no message handler attached to an option, the menu option will be greyed out.

Resource editors

The Accelerator, Dialog, Menu and Version editors were discussed earlier. The other editors are briefly described here.

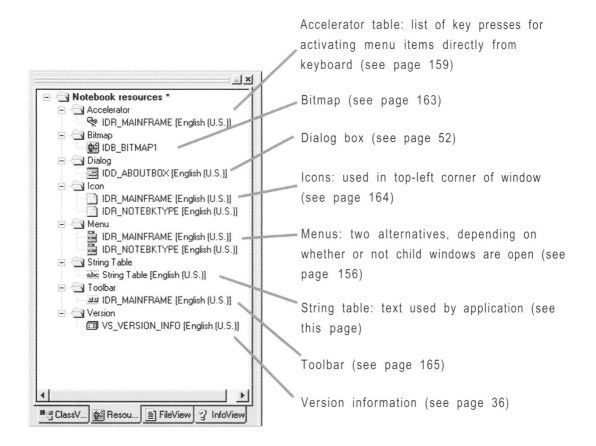

Accelerator table: list of key presses for activating menu items directly from keyboard (see page 159)

Bitmap (see page 163)

Dialog box (see page 52)

Icons: used in top-left corner of window (see page 164)

Menus: two alternatives, depending on whether or not child windows are open (see page 156)

String table: text used by application (see this page)

Toolbar (see page 165)

Version information (see page 36)

String tables

The string table stores the strings that are used by the application for displaying help text on the status bar. These have already been set up for the standard menu options but new strings can be added for the extra options.

In ResourceView, open the String Table and double-click on the String Table entry (there is only one for each application). The string table editor is displayed.

161

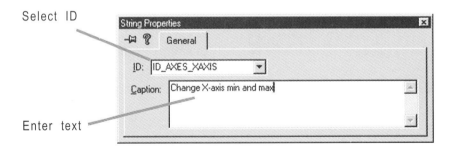

ID	Value	Caption
IDR_MAINFRAME	128	Notebook
IDR_NOTEBKTYPE	129	\nNotebk\nNotebk\nNotebook Files (*.nbk)\n.nbk\nNotebook.Do
ID_AXES_YAXIS	32773	Change Y-axis min and max
AFX_IDS_APP_TITLE	57344	Notebook
AFX_IDS_IDLEMESSAGE	57345	For Help, press F1
AFX_IDS_HELPMODEMESSA	57346	Select an object on which to get Help
ID_FILE_NEW	57600	Create a new document\nNew
ID_FILE_OPEN	57601	Open an existing document\nOpen
ID_FILE_CLOSE	57602	Close the active document\nClose
ID_FILE_SAVE	57603	Save the active document\nSave
ID_FILE_SAVE_AS	57604	Save the active document with a new name\nSave As
ID_FILE_PAGE_SETUP	57605	Change the printing options\nPage Setup
ID_FILE_PRINT_SETUP	57606	Change the printer and printing options\nPrint Setup
ID_FILE_PRINT	57607	Print the active document\nPrint
ID_FILE_PRINT_PREVIEW	57609	Display full pages\nPrint Preview
ID_FILE_MRU_FILE1	57616	Open this document
ID_FILE_MRU_FILE2	57617	Open this document
ID_FILE_MRU_FILE3	57618	Open this document
ID_FILE_MRU_FILE4	57619	Open this document
ID_FILE_MRU_FILE5	57620	Open this document
ID_FILE_MRU_FILE6	57621	Open this document
ID_FILE_MRU_FILE7	57622	Open this document
ID_FILE_MRU_FILE8	57623	Open this document

To add a new string, double-click on the blank line at the bottom of the table; the String Properties box is displayed.

Choose the ID for the required option and then enter the text that you wish to see on the status line. Press **[Enter]** when the text is complete.

Select ID

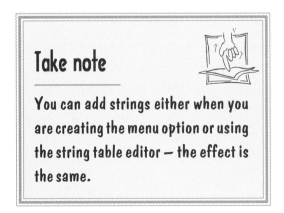

Enter text

Take note

You can add strings either when you are creating the menu option or using the string table editor — the effect is the same.

Tip

To change a string, double-click on the line in the table and then edit the text in the Properties box.

162

Bitmaps

Bitmaps can be used in several ways; for instance, you may want to add a picture control that displays a bitmap or replace an ordinary command button with a bitmap button.

When you open the Bitmap folder in ResourceView there is a single (empty) bitmap; IDB_BITMAP1. You can create further bitmaps by right-clicking on the folder and selecting Insert Bitmap.

Double-clicking on a bitmap ID opens the bitmap editor.

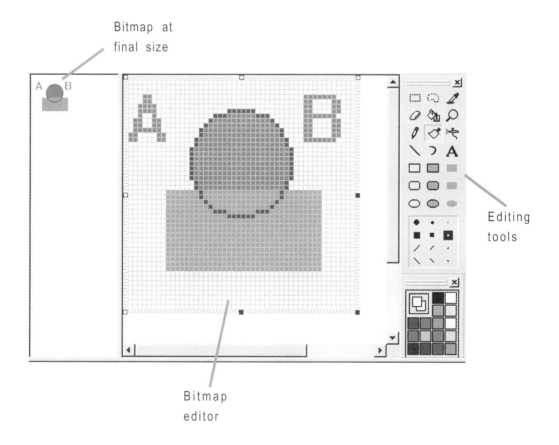

Bitmap at final size

Editing tools

Bitmap editor

All the usual Paint-type tools are available for editing the bitmap, pixel by pixel. As you edit the bitmap, a small picture shows the bitmap as it will appear on screen.

To include the bitmap on a dialog box, add a picture control and change its Image property to the bitmap's ID.

Take note

Bitmap buttons need up to four different bitmaps, one for each of the four possible states of a button: button up, button down, focussed and disabled.

For information on adding a bitmap button, search on-line help for CBitmapButton.

Tip

You can also import bitmaps from other sources by selecting Import from the right-click menu and listing all files. If used for a picture control, the control will expand to fit the bitmap.

Icons

The icon editor works in a similar way to the bitmap editor.

By default, the application includes two icons:

IDR_MAINFRAME   The icon used for the control-menu button, the taskbar and the About box

IDR_*name*TYPE   The document icon used on the child windows

You can also add other icons for use in your application.

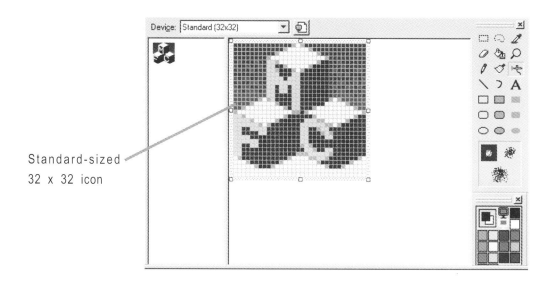

Standard-sized
32 x 32 icon

The icon can be edited pixel by pixel, using the tools from the toolbox on the right. The finished icon is shown in the top left corner of the editor.

Toolbars

The application has a single toolbar, IDR_MAINFRAME, which is displayed at the top of the main window on SDI and MDI applications.

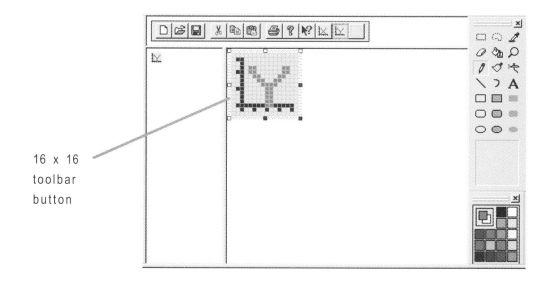

16 x 16
toolbar
button

Tip

You can separate groups of buttons with a thin space by dragging a button only halfway into the gap between groups. To close up a gap, drag a button so that it slightly overlaps its neighbour.

Tip

To delete a toolbar button, drag it off the toolbar onto the editor window.

The buttons are used as shortcuts to menu options (or may be totally independent of all other options).

The toolbar editor is a variation of the icon editor. The toolbar is displayed at the top of the editor and clicking on any button allows you to edit it, pixel by pixel.

New buttons are added by clicking on the blank item on the right of the toolbar. The order of the buttons can be changed by dragging the buttons along the toolbar.

You can add message handlers to a toolbar button in two ways:

- Use View | Properties to change the ID of the button to that of an existing ID (e.g. a menu option ID). When clicked, the button will then automatically call the same message handler as the matching menu option.

- Use View | Properties to give the button a different ID and then use ClassWizard to create a message handler for the COMMAND message. The function is then completed in the usual way.

The toolbar button is greyed out until a handler is attached in one these ways.

166

Printing

If you want to print single-page documents, there is very little you have to do to implement printer-handling functions. AppWizard adds all the necessary functions (unless you specify otherwise) when the application is created. Therefore you will find that the Print, Print Preview and Print Setup options all work in the usual way.

The Print dialog box is fully functional and needs no further adjustment. The entire document is printed when you click on OK; alternatively, clicking on the printer button on the toolbar will print the whole document without displaying the dialog box.

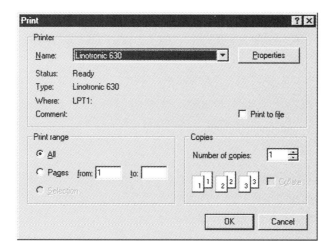

Standard Print dialog box

The Print Setup box is the same as would be found on any Windows application and can be left as it is.

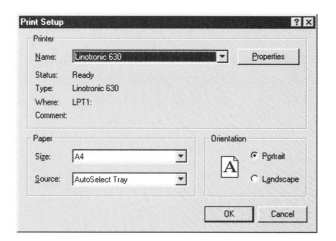

Print Setup dialog box

The Print Preview dialog has all the usual buttons and gives an indication of what the printed document will look like.

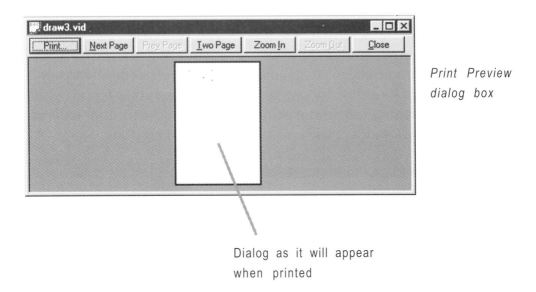

Print Preview dialog box

Dialog as it will appear when printed

It becomes apparent immediately that the printed version of the document will be very small (depending on the resolution of the printer). In order to print at a reasonable size, you will probably need to change the mapping mode. This is done using the SetMapMode function. For example:

```
pDC->SetMapMode(LOENGLISH);
```

This changes the physical units from pixels to 0.01 inches and is the largest scale of the standard mapping modes. The SetMapMode function can be called from within the OnDraw function. Remember that most modes have their origin at the bottom left corner of the window, rather than the top left; therefore, you will also need to reverse the direction of the y co-ordinates.

Print functions

AppWizard includes three empty print functions in the view source file. These are shown below.

Print functions

```
/////////////////////////////////////////////////////////////////////////////
// CVisDrawView  printing

BOOL    CVisDrawView::OnPreparePrinting(CPrintInfo*    pInfo)
{
    // default preparation
    return    DoPreparePrinting(pInfo);
}

void  CVisDrawView::OnBeginPrinting(CDC*  /*pDC*/, CPrintInfo*  /
*pInfo*/)
{
    // TODO: add extra initialization before printing
}

void  CVisDrawView::OnEndPrinting(CDC*  /*pDC*/, CPrintInfo*  /
*pInfo*/)
{
    // TODO: add cleanup after printing
}
```

The functions have the following uses:

- The **OnPreparePrinting** function carries out any necessary preparatory work before the document is previewed or printed.

- Further initialisation is carried out in **OnBeginPrinting**, which is called just before printing takes place. This function has a pointer to the CDC object as one of its parameters so any changes to the device context should be made here.

- **OnEndPrinting** can be used for any tidying up after printing has finished. For example, you may want to restore the device context attributes to the values they had when OnBeginPrinting was called.

For multi-page printing a little more work is necessary; search the on-line help for 'Printing multipage documents'.

Help options

If you selected the help options when creating the application, AppWizard will have set up a help application for you. The files used in the on-line help are listed in the Help folder in ResourceView. These include:

- AfxCore.rtf, a basic help file covering all the standard features that have been added to the application

- AfxPrint.rtf, a similar document for the print options (not all applications include the print options, so this file may be omitted)

- A selection of bitmap files that are used to illustrate the help file

- Control files for creating the help file

If you select Help | Contents you will be able to inspect the standard help file. This has topics for each menu item, with suggestions for those places where you can add or delete text.

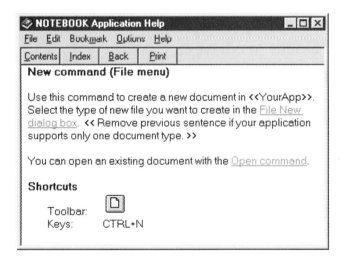

The AfxCore.rtf is the source of this text and can be opened in Word. By comparing the compiled help file with the RTF file, the way in which the file is structured should begin to become apparent.

Footnotes are used for very specific purposes within the text:

- The # footnote identifies a context label, which identifies a particular help topic.

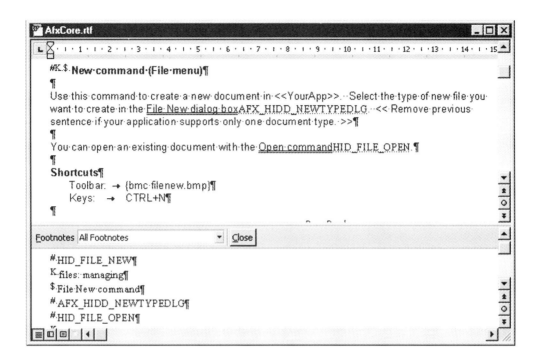

- The $ footnote marks a title string, which is used as a bookmark, in the history list and in the bottom half of the Index window.

- The K footnote is followed by a list of keywords; these are the words and phrases that are included in the Index list.

Other footnote symbols are used for browsing sequences and compilation options.

Within the text itself, the hypertext links are marked as follows:

- For jumps to other topics, the text to be highlighted is marked with a double-underline style and is immediately followed by the context label to jump to, formatted as hidden text.

- For glossary entries, the text itself has a single underline and is again followed by the context label (as hidden text).

You can include bitmaps by specifying the file in the format {bmc *filename*.bmp}.

This information should be enough for you to modify the help file to suit your own application. To supply more detailed help, search on-line help for 'Context-sensitive help' and choose the appropriate Help Topic.

Exercises

1   Add a new menu to the VisDraw main menu. The menu should be called Attributes, with an access key of a 'a', and should be between Window and Help.

The menu should contain a single item, Change, with access key 'c' and accelerator **[Ctrl-A]**.

When the menu option is clicked it should display the Line-drawing Features dialog box (which should not be displayed when the program is first run). This allows the attributes to be changed more than once; the attributes should be saved along with the rest of the data.

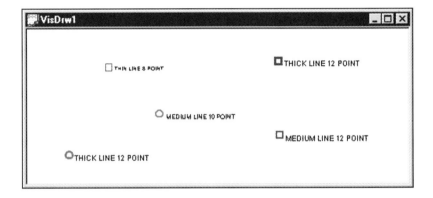

2   Print a document from VisDraw and save the document. Change the application so that it uses the LOENGLISH mapping mode and print again.

3   Adapt the help file to suit the VisDraw application.

For solutions to these exercises, see page 190.

172

9 Solutions to exercises

1 Overview (p10)

1 Click on the Start button, Programs, Microsoft Visual C++ folder and Visual C++ application icon.

The main window (including title bar, menu bar, toolbars and status bar), Project Workspace window (with InfoView tab), InfoViewer floating toolbar and help window should be visible (the exact composition of the display will depend on how the environment was left when you last exited the program).

2 Close the Project Workspace window, floating toolbars and help window by clicking on the Close button. Redisplay the Project Workspace by selecting Help | Contents; redisplay the help window by selecting the first topic in the InfoViewer tree; re-instate the toolbars by selecting Tools | Customize, clicking on the Toolbars tab and clicking on the required toolbars.

Move the Project Workspace window and toolbars by dragging any unused area to a new position. Dock toolbars by dragging their title bars to an edge of the main window. Resize windows by dragging their edges and corners.

Minimise the windows by clicking on their Minimise button; restore the help window by clicking on the Minimise button; restore the help window by clicking on the Minimise button on the minimised icon; restore the main window by clicking on the Visual C++ taskbar button.

3 Click on the Search button on the InfoViewer toolbar (or select Help | Search); type 'infov'; select 'InfoViewer, choosing as Web browser'. (Note that you cannot get to this topic by searching on 'internet' or 'www' but 'web' does lead to the same place.)

2 Applications (p26)

1 Select File | New, click on the Projects tab and on MFC AppWizard (exe). Type 'VisDraw' for the Project Name; click on OK. Click on Next at steps 1, 2 and 3.

At step 4, click on Context-Sensitive Help. Click on the Advanced button; enter 'vid' as the File Extension, 'Visual C++ Draw' as the Main Frame Caption and 'VisDraw' as the Doc Type Name. Enter 'Visual C++ Draw Files (*.vid)' (or something similar) for the Filter Name and 'Visual C++ Draw document' for the long file name. Accept the options at step 5, click on Finish at step 6 and click on OK on the summary screen.

2 Select Build | Execute VisDraw.exe of press **[Ctrl-F5]**. Confirm that the EXE file is to be built. All standard Windows functionality should be available when the program runs (as described on pp21-22). Click on the Close button to end the application.

3 Select File | New, click on the Projects tab and on MFC AppWizard (exe). Type 'VisCalc' for the Project Name and click on OK.

At Step 1, click on Dialog Based and then on Next. At step 2, enter 'Visual C++ Calculator' as the Title.

2   Applications (continued)

Accept the defaults for step 3, click on Finish at step 4 and OK on the summary.

4. Press **[Ctrl-F5]** to build and run the application. Click on OK to close it down.

3   Exploring the application (p50)

1 Use File | Recent Workspaces to load VisDraw. Click on the ClassView to list the classes. To check on the base class for a class, double-click on the class and look for a statement near the top of the header file such as:

```
class CChildFrame : public CMDIChild
```

The classes in VisDraw are:

CChildFrame	base class CMDIChildWnd
CMainFrame	base class CMDIFrameWnd
CVisDrawApp	base class CWinApp
CVisDrawDoc	base class CDocument
CVisDrawView	base class CView

2 Click on ResourceView, open the Version folder and double-click on VS_VERSION_INFO. Double-click on the items to be changed and enter the new information. Click on the Close box when the changes are complete, then save the changes with File | Save All.

3 In ClassView, open CVisDrawApp and double-click on InitInstance (or double-click on VisDraw.cpp in the Source Files folder of FileView). Find the SetRegistryKey function call and change the text in the quotes to your name or your company's name. For example:

```
SetRegistryKey(_T("Southbury   Software"));
```

Close the editor window by clicking on the Close button and click on Yes to save the changes.

4   Dialog boxes (p66)

1 Open VisDraw. Select Insert | Resource (or press **[Ctrl-R]**) and double-click on the Dialog option. Right-click and select Properties from the menu. Replace the ID with 'IDD_LINESDIALOG' and the Caption with 'Line-drawing features'. Press **[Enter]**. Save the changes with File | Save All.

2 Press **[Ctrl-W]** to invoke the ClassWizard. Click on OK to add a new class. Type 'CLinesDialog' as the Name and click on OK. Click on OK again to close ClassWizard.

3 Open VisDraw.cpp. At the bottom of the block of #include statements add the following line:

```
#include  "LinesDialog.h"
```

4 Dialog boxes (continued)

In InitInstance, replace the 'return TRUE' statement at the end of the function with the following:

```
CLinesDialog dlg;
if (dlg.DoModal() == IDOK)
{
    return TRUE;    // OK pressed
}
else
{
    return FALSE;   // Cancel pressed
}
```

Press **[Ctrl-F5]** to build and run the application. Pressing OK on the dialog box should allow the application to continue while Cancel should close it down.

5 Dialog controls (p94)

(Note that the dimensions given below are suggested values only.)

1   Turn the grid on to make it easier to position controls. The dialog has the following properties:

Width x Height:	182 x 126

The controls have the following properties:

Labels

ID:	IDC_STATIC_LINESIZE	IDC_STATIC_FONT
Caption:	Line thickness:	Text font:
Align Text:	Right	Right
Left, Top:	30, 35	30, 65
Width x Height:	50 x 10	50 x 10

ID:	IDC_STATIC_CURRENT
Caption:	Current settings:
Align Text:	Center
Left, Top:	20, 10
Width x Height:	135 x 10

Combo boxes

ID:	IDC_COMBO_LINESIZE	IDC_COMBO_FONT
Sort:	Off	Off
Type:	Dropdown	Dropdown
Left, Top:	90, 35	90, 65
Width x Height:	48 x 48	48 x 48

5   Dialog controls (continued)

Command Buttons

ID:	IDOK	IDCANCEL
Caption:	OK	Cancel
Default Button:	On	Off

To test the dialog box, click on the left-hand button on the Dialog toolbar. Use File | Save to save the changes.

2   Open the VisCalc application (File | Recent Workspaces). In ResourceView open the dialog folder and double-click on IDD_VISCALC_DIALOG.

Turn the grid on.

The dialog box has the following properties:

Labels

ID:	IDC_STATIC_FIRST	ID_STATIC_SECOND
Caption:	First value:	Second value:
Align Text:	Right	Right
Left, Top:	10, 20	10, 40
Width x Height:	55 x 10	55 x 10

ID:	IDC_STATIC_RESULT
Caption:	Result:
Align Text:	Right
Left, Top:	10, 80
Width x Height:	55 x 10

Edit boxes

ID:	IDC_EDIT_FIRST	IDC_EDIT_SECOND
Number:	On	On
Disabled:	Off	Off
Left, Top:	75, 20	75, 40
Width x Height:	55 x 14	55 x 14

ID:	IDC_EDIT_RESULT
Number:	Off
Disabled:	On
Left, Top:	75, 80
Width x Height:	55 x 14

Command buttons

ID:	IDC_BUTTON_ADD	IDC_BUTTON_SUB
Caption:	+	-
Disabled:	Off	Off
Default Button:	Off	Off
Left, Top:	145, 20	171, 20
Width x Height:	20 x 20	20 x 20

ID:	IDC_BUTTON_MULT	IDC_BUTTON_DIV
Caption:	*	/
Disabled:	Off	Off
Default Button:	Off	Off
Left, Top:	145, 45	171, 45
Width x Height:	20 x 20	20 x 20

ID:	IDC_BUTTON_CLEAR	IDC_BUTTON_COPY
Caption:	CLEAR ALL	Copy Result to First Value
Disabled:	On	On
Default Button:	Off	Off
Left, Top:	205, 20	145, 80
Width x Height:	45 x 45	105 x 14

ID:	IDOK
Caption:	END PROGRAM
Disabled:	Off
Default Button:	On
Left, Top:	105, 110
Width x Height:	70 x 14

Delete the Cancel button (click on it and press **[Del]**).

Press **[Ctrl-F5]** to run the program. This will also save the changes. Click on END PROGRAM to close down the program.

6 Events and functions (p124)

1   Display the dialog box and press **[Ctrl-W]** to invoke the ClassWizard. Click on the Member Variables tab. Enter a variable name of m_comboLineSize, with Category 'Control'. Repeat for IDC_COMBO_FONT, giving it a name of m_comboFont, with Category 'Control'.

For IDC_STATIC_CURRENT, add a member variable named m_staticCurrent, of type CString.

Click on the Message Maps tab. Click on CLinesDialog for the Object ID and WM_SHOWWINDOW for the message. Click on Add Function, then on Edit Code. Amend the function as shown below.

Add functions for the CBN_KILLFOCUS message for both IDC_COMBO_LINESIZE and IDC_COMBO_FONT. Edit the functions as shown below.

In ClassView, right-click on CLinesDialog and select Add Member Function. Give the function a Function Type of 'void', a Function Declaration of ShowCurrentSettings and Access type of Protected. Fill in the function as shown below.

Lines Dialog.cpp should be as follows:

```
// LinesDialog.cpp : implementation file
//

#include  "stdafx.h"
#include  "VisDraw.h"
#include  "LinesDialog.h"

#ifdef  _DEBUG
#define  new  DEBUG_NEW
#undef  THIS_FILE
static char THIS_FILE[] = __FILE__;
#endif

/////////////////////////////////////////////////////////////////////////////
// CLinesDialog dialog

CLinesDialog::CLinesDialog(CWnd*  pParent  /*=NULL*/)
    : CDialog(CLinesDialog::IDD, pParent)
{
    //{{AFX_DATA_INIT(CLinesDialog)
    m_staticCurrent = _T("");
    m_comboFont = _T("");
    m_comboLineSize = _T("");
    //}}AFX_DATA_INIT
}

void  CLinesDialog::DoDataExchange(CDataExchange*  pDX)
{
    CDialog::DoDataExchange(pDX);
    //{{AFX_DATA_MAP(CLinesDialog)
    DDX_Control(pDX, IDC_COMBO_LINESIZE, m_CcomboLineSize);
    DDX_Control(pDX, IDC_COMBO_FONT, m_CcomboFont);
    DDX_Text(pDX, IDC_STATIC_CURRENT, m_staticCurrent);
    DDX_CBString(pDX, IDC_COMBO_FONT, m_comboFont);
    DDX_CBString(pDX, IDC_COMBO_LINESIZE, m_comboLineSize);
    //}}AFX_DATA_MAP
}

BEGIN_MESSAGE_MAP(CLinesDialog,  CDialog)
    //{{AFX_MSG_MAP(CLinesDialog)
    ON_WM_SHOWWINDOW()
    ON_CBN_KILLFOCUS(IDC_COMBO_LINESIZE,
        OnKillfocusComboLinesize)
```

```
        ON_CBN_KILLFOCUS(IDC_COMBO_FONT,          OnKillfocusComboFont)
        //}}AFX_MSG_MAP
    END_MESSAGE_MAP()

    /////////////////////////////////////////////////////////////////////////////
    // CLinesDialog message handlers

    void CLinesDialog::OnShowWindow(BOOL bShow, UINT nStatus)
    {
        CDialog::OnShowWindow(bShow,    nStatus);

        m_CcomboLineSize.AddString("Thin    line");
        m_CcomboLineSize.AddString("Medium    line");
        m_CcomboLineSize.AddString("Thick    line");
        m_CcomboLineSize.SetCurSel(0);

        m_CcomboFont.AddString("8    point");
        m_CcomboFont.AddString("10    point");
        m_CcomboFont.AddString("12    point");
        m_CcomboFont.SetCurSel(0);

        ShowCurrentSettings();
    }

    void    CLinesDialog::OnKillfocusComboLinesize()
    {
        ShowCurrentSettings();
    }

    void    CLinesDialog::OnKillfocusComboFont()
    {
        ShowCurrentSettings();
    }

    void    CLinesDialog::ShowCurrentSettings()
    {
        UpdateData();               // Get data from dialog
        m_staticCurrent = "Current settings: " + m_comboLineSize
            + ", " + m_comboFont + " text";
        UpdateData(FALSE);       // Update dialog data
    }
```

6 Events and functions (continued)

2 Using ClassWizard, add the following member variables:

IDC_EDIT_FIRST	m_editFirst	Type: float
IDC_EDIT_SECOND	m_editSecond	Type: float
IDC_EDIT_RESULT	m_editResult	Type: float
IDC_EDIT_SECOND	m_CeditSecond	Type: CEdit
IDC_BUTTON_CLEAR	m_btnClear	Type: CButton
IDC_BUTTON_COPY	m_btnCopy	Type: CButton

Add the following message handlers:

IDC_EDIT_FIRST	EN_KILLFOCUS
IDC_EDIT_SECOND	EN_KILLFOCUS
IDC_BUTTON_ADD	BN_CLICKED
IDC_BUTTON_SUB	BN_CLICKED
IDC_BUTTON_MULT	BN_CLICKED
IDC_BUTTON_DIV	BN_CLICKED
IDC_BUTTON_CLEAR	BN_CLICKED
IDC_BUTTON_COPY	BN_CLICKED

The new message handlers are as follows:

```
void    CVisCalcDlg::OnKillfocusEditFirst()
{
    float orig = m_editFirst;   // Store original value

    UpdateData(TRUE);           // Retrieve data from dialog box
    if (orig != m_editFirst)    // Value has changed
    {
        m_editResult = 0;              // Clear results box
        UpdateData(FALSE);

        m_btnClear.EnableWindow(TRUE);
        m_btnCopy.EnableWindow(FALSE);
    }
}

void    CVisCalcDlg::OnKillfocusEditSecond()
{
    float orig = m_editSecond;

    UpdateData(TRUE);
    if (orig != m_editSecond)
    {
        m_editResult = 0;
        UpdateData(FALSE);
        m_btnClear.EnableWindow(TRUE);
```

```
            m_btnCopy.EnableWindow(FALSE);
    }
}
void    CVisCalcDlg::OnButtonAdd()
{
    UpdateData(TRUE);       // Retrieve data from dialog box
    m_editResult = m_editFirst + m_editSecond;
    UpdateData(FALSE);      // Update dialog with result
    m_btnCopy.EnableWindow(TRUE);
}

void    CVisCalcDlg::OnButtonSub()
{
    UpdateData(TRUE);
    m_editResult = m_editFirst - m_editSecond;
    UpdateData(FALSE);
    m_btnCopy.EnableWindow(TRUE);
}

void    CVisCalcDlg::OnButtonMult()
{
    UpdateData(TRUE);
    m_editResult = m_editFirst * m_cditSccond;
    UpdateData(FALSE);
    m_btnCopy.EnableWindow(TRUE);
}

void    CVisCalcDlg::OnButtonDiv()
{
    UpdateData(TRUE);       // Retrieve data from dialog box

    if (m_editSecond != 0)    // Check that divisor is not zero
    {
        m_editResult = m_editFirst / m_editSecond;
        UpdateData(FALSE);
        m_btnCopy.EnableWindow(TRUE);
    }
    else // Zero divisor, so put cursor back on box
    {
        m_CeditSecond.SetFocus();
    }
}
```

6   Events and functions (continued)

```
void     CVisCalcDlg::OnButtonClear()
{
        m_editFirst  =  0;
        m_editSecond  =  0;
        m_editResult  =  0;
        UpdateData(FALSE);  //  All  boxes  set  to  zero
        m_btnClear.EnableWindow(FALSE);
        m_btnCopy.EnableWindow(FALSE);
}

void     CVisCalcDlg::OnButtonCopy()
{
        UpdateData(TRUE);
        m_editFirst  =  m_editResult;   //  Copy  result  to  first  box
        m_editSecond  =  0;
        m_editResult  =  0;
        UpdateData(FALSE);
        m_btnCopy.EnableWindow(FALSE);
}
```

7   Documents and views (p150)

1   Add the following member variable declarations in VisDrawDoc.h:

public:
```
UINT   ShapeIndex;
CPoint   ShapePos[100];
UINT   ShapeSquare[100];
```

Add the following line in CVisDrawDoc::OnNewDocument:

```
ShapeIndex  =  0;
```

Add the following message handlers for the CVisDrawView Object ID:

```
WM_LBUTTONDOWN
WM_RBUTTONDOWN
```

Change the message handlers as follows:

```
void   CVisDrawView::OnDraw(CDC*   pDC)
{
    CVisDrawDoc*  pDoc  =  GetDocument();
    ASSERT_VALID(pDoc);

    UINT  x1,  y1,  x2,  y2;

    UINT  MaxIndex  =  pDoc->ShapeIndex;
```

7   Documents and views (continued)

```
                    for (UINT i = 0; i < MaxIndex; ++i)
                    {
                        x1 = pDoc->ShapePos[i].x;
                        y1 = pDoc->ShapePos[i].y;
                        x2 = x1 + 10;
                        y2 = y1 + 10;
                        if (pDoc->ShapeSquare[i] == 1)
                        {
                         CPen NewPen(PS_SOLID, 1, RGB(0, 0, 255));
                         pDC->SelectObject(&NewPen);
                         pDC->Rectangle(x1, y1, x2, y2);
                        }
                        else
                        {
                         CPen NewPen(PS_SOLID, 1, RGB(255, 0, 0));
                         pDC->SelectObject(&NewPen);
                         pDC->Ellipse(x1, y1, x2, y2);
                        }
                    }
                }

                void CVisDrawView::OnLButtonDown(UINT nFlags, CPoint point)
                {
                    CVisDrawDoc* pDoc = GetDocument();

                    if (pDoc->ShapeIndex >= 100)
                        return;

                    pDoc->ShapePos[pDoc->ShapeIndex] = point;
                    pDoc->ShapeSquare[pDoc->ShapeIndex] = 1;  // Draw square
                    pDoc->ShapeIndex++;
                    pDoc->SetModifiedFlag();
                    Invalidate();

                    CView::OnLButtonDown(nFlags,   point);
                }

                void CVisDrawView::OnRButtonDown(UINT nFlags, CPoint point)
                {
                    CVisDrawDoc* pDoc = GetDocument();
                    if (pDoc->ShapeIndex >= 100)
                        return;

                    pDoc->ShapePos[pDoc->ShapeIndex] = point;
                    pDoc->ShapeSquare[pDoc->ShapeIndex] = 0;  // Draw circle
```

```
                    pDoc->ShapeIndex++;

                    pDoc->SetModifiedFlag();
                    Invalidate();

                    CView::OnRButtonDown(nFlags,   point);
                }
```

2   Add the following public member variable declaration in VisDrawDoc.h:

```
        CString   ShapeText[100];
```

Add the following message handler for CVisDrawView:

```
        WM_KEYDOWN
```

Change the message handlers as follows:

```
    void  CVisDrawView::OnDraw(CDC*  pDC)
    {
        CVisDrawDoc* pDoc = GetDocument();
        ASSERT_VALID(pDoc);

        UINT x1, y1, x2, y2, x3, y3;                // Add new variables

        UINT MaxIndex = pDoc->ShapeIndex;

        for (UINT i = 0; i < MaxIndex; ++i)
        {
            x1 = pDoc->ShapePos[i].x;
            y1 = pDoc->ShapePos[i].y;

            x2 = x1 + 10;
            y2 = y1 + 10;

            x3 = x2 + 3;                   // Set variable values
            y3 = y1 - 3;

            if (pDoc->ShapeSquare[i] == 1)
            {
             CPen NewPen(PS_SOLID, 1, RGB(0, 0, 255));
             pDC->SelectObject(&NewPen);

             pDC->Rectangle(x1, y1, x2, y2);
            }
            else
```

```
            {
              CPen NewPen(PS_SOLID, 1, RGB(255, 0, 0));
              pDC->SelectObject(&NewPen);

              pDC->Ellipse(x1, y1, x2, y2);
            }
            pDC->TextOut(x3, y3, pDoc->ShapeText[i]); // Show text
        }
}

void CVisDrawView::OnKeyDown(UINT nChar, UINT nRepCnt, UINT nFlags)
{
    CVisDrawDoc* pDoc = GetDocument();

    pDoc->ShapeText[pDoc->ShapeIndex - 1] += nChar;  // Store next letter

    pDoc->SetModifiedFlag();
    Invalidate();                        // Display text so far

    CView::OnKeyDown(nChar, nRepCnt, nFlags);
}
```

3   Amend CVisDrawDoc::Serialize as follows:

```
void CVisDrawDoc::Serialize(CArchive& ar)
{
    if (ar.IsStoring())              //storing data
    {
        for (UINT i = 0; i < ShapeIndex; ++i)
        {
          ar << ShapePos[i].x;
          ar << ShapePos[i].y;
          ar << ShapeSquare[i];
          ar << ShapeText[i];
        }
        ar << -1;
    }
    else                     //loading data
    {
        int x1 = 0;
        ShapeIndex = 0;

        while (x1 != -1)
        {
          ar >> x1;
```

```
                    if  (x1  !=  -1)
                    {
                            ShapePos[ShapeIndex].x  =  x1;
                            ar  >>  ShapePos[ShapeIndex].y;
                            ar  >>  ShapeSquare[ShapeIndex];
                            ar  >>  ShapeText[ShapeIndex];
                            ShapeIndex++;
                    }
                }
            }
        }
```

4   Add two edit boxes to the Line-drawing Features dialog box and attach the following variables to them:

IDC_EDIT_LINESIZE	m_editLineSize	Type: UINT
IDC_EDIT_FONTSIZE	m_editFontSize	Type: UINT

The Visible property should be turned off in both cases.

In LinesDialog.cpp, change ShowCurrentSettings as follows:

```
void    CLinesDialog::ShowCurrentSettings()
{
    UpdateData();               // Get data from dialog
    m_staticCurrent = "Current settings: " + m_comboLineSize
        + ", " + m_comboFont + " text";

    // Get 0, 1 or 2 from LineSize box and convert to 1, 2 or 3
    m_editLineSize = m_CcomboLineSize.GetCurSel() + 1;

    // Get 0, 1 or 2 from FontSize box and convert to 8, 10 or 12
    m_editFontSize = (m_CcomboFont.GetCurSel() * 2) + 8;

    UpdateData(FALSE);      // Update dialog data
}
```

(This retrieves the settings from the combo boxes and stores them in the hidden edit boxes.)

Add the following variables to VisDrawView.h:

```
public:
    UINT  FontSize;
    UINT  LineSize;
```

Add the following function:

```
protected:
    void  SetUpFont(CDC*  pDC,  UINT  FontSize);
```

The function is defined as follows:

```
void  CVisDrawView::SetUpFont(CDC*  pDC,  UINT  FontSize)
{
    LOGFONT   NewFont;

    NewFont.lfHeight  =  FontSize;
    NewFont.lfWidth  =  0;
    NewFont.lfEscapement  =  0;
    NewFont.lfOrientation  =  0;
    NewFont.lfWeight  =  0;
    NewFont.lfItalic  =  0;
    NewFont.lfUnderline  =  0;
    NewFont.lfStrikeOut  =  0;
    NewFont.lfCharSet  =  ANSI_CHARSET;
    NewFont.lfOutPrecision  =  OUT_DEFAULT_PRECIS;
    NewFont.lfClipPrecision  =  CLIP_DEFAULT_PRECIS;
    NewFont.lfQuality  =  DEFAULT_QUALITY;
    NewFont.lfPitchAndFamily  =  DEFAULT_PITCH  |  FF_MODERN;
    strcpy(NewFont.lfFaceName,   "Arial");

    CFont   FontObj;
    FontObj.CreateFontIndirect(&NewFont);
    pDC->SelectObject(&FontObj);
}
```

(This function changes the font to that given in FontSize.)

At the top of the source file, insert:

```
#include  "LinesDialog.h"
```

Amend the OnDraw function as follows:

```
void  CVisDrawView::OnDraw(CDC*  pDC)
{
    CVisDrawDoc*  pDoc  =  GetDocument();
    ASSERT_VALID(pDoc);

    if  (LineSize  ==  0)
    {
        CLinesDialog  dlg;

        dlg.DoModal();
```

```
            LineSize  =  dlg.m_editLineSize;
            FontSize  =  dlg.m_editFontSize;
    }

    UINT  x1,  y1,  x2,  y2,  x3,  y3;

    UINT  MaxIndex  =  pDoc->ShapeIndex;

    for  (UINT  i = 0;  i < MaxIndex;  ++i)
    {
        x1  =  pDoc->ShapePos[i].x;
        y1  =  pDoc->ShapePos[i].y;

        x2 = x1 + 10;
        y2 = y1 + 10;

        x3 = x2 + 3;
        y3 = y1 - 3;

        if  (pDoc->ShapeSquare[i]  ==  1)
        {
          CPen  NewPen(PS_SOLID,  LineSize,  RGB(0,  0,  255));
          pDC->SelectObject(&NewPen);

          pDC->Rectangle(x1,  y1,  x2,  y2);
        }
        else
        {
          CPen  NewPen(PS_SOLID,  LineSize,  RGB(255,  0,  0));
          pDC->SelectObject(&NewPen);

          pDC->Ellipse(x1,  y1,  x2,  y2);
        }

        SetUpFont(pDC,    FontSize);
        pDC->TextOut(x3,   y3,   pDoc->ShapeText[i]);
    }
}
```

(The dialog box is now called when the window is first drawn and the DC attributes are set accordingly.)

In VisDraw.cpp, remove the following line:

```
#include  "LinesDialog.h"
```

7 Documents and views (continued)

At the end of InitInstance, remove the lines beginning 'CLinesDialog dlg' and replace them with:

```
return  TRUE;
```

(This stops the dialog from being called at this stage.)

8 Programming options (p172)

1   In ResourceView, open the Menu folder and double-click on IDR_VISDRWTYPE. Double-click to the right of Help and enter '&Attributes' for the Caption.

Double-click below Attributes and enter '&Change' for the Caption. Drag the Attributes menu between Window and Help.

Open the Accelerator folder and double-click on IDR_MAINFRAME. Double-click on the blank line at the bottom and enter the following properties:

ID:	ID_ATTRIBUTES_CHANGE
Key:	A
Ctrl:	On

Save all files.

In ClasWizard, select the CVisDrawView class and add the following function:

Object ID:	ID_ATTRIBUTES_CHANGE
Message:	COMMAND

The function should be as follows:

```
void    CVisDrawView::OnAttributesChange()
{
    CLinesDialog  dlg;

    dlg.DoModal();

    LineSize  =  dlg.m_editLineSize;
    FontSize  =  dlg.m_editFontSize;
}
```

The code is moved from OnDraw.

The OnKeyDown function should be changed so that it ignores control characters:

```
void  CVisDrawView::OnKeyDown(UINT  nChar,  UINT  nRepCnt,  UINT  nFlags)
{
    CVisDrawDoc*  pDoc  =  GetDocument();
```

```
            if (nChar > 31)
            {
                pDoc->ShapeText[pDoc->ShapeIndex - 1] += nChar;

                pDoc->SetModifiedFlag();
                Invalidate();
            }

            CView::OnKeyDown(nChar,  nRepCnt,  nFlags);
        }
```

The following public declarations must be added to VisDrawDoc.h:

```
UINT   ShapeLine[100];
UINT   ShapeFont[100];
```

The following functions should be changed in VisDrawView.cpp:

```
BOOL   CVisDrawView::PreCreateWindow(CREATESTRUCT&   cs)
{
    LineSize = 1;       // Set line and font defaults
    FontSize = 8;

    return   CView::PreCreateWindow(cs);
}

void  CVisDrawView::OnDraw(CDC*  pDC)
{
    CVisDrawDoc* pDoc = GetDocument();
    ASSERT_VALID(pDoc);

    // Delete lines from here

    UINT x1, y1, x2, y2, x3, y3;
    UINT LS, FS;       // New variables

    UINT MaxIndex = pDoc->ShapeIndex;
    for (UINT i = 0; i < MaxIndex; ++i)
    {
        x1 = pDoc->ShapePos[i].x;
        y1 = pDoc->ShapePos[i].y;

        x2 = x1 + 10;
        y2 = y1 + 10;

        x3 = x2 + 3;
        y3 = y1 - 3;
```

8   Programming options (continued)

```
                LS = pDoc->ShapeLine[i];   // Set values of variables
                FS = pDoc->ShapeFont[i];

                if (pDoc->ShapeSquare[i] == 1)
                {
                 // Set line size for each symbol separately
                 CPen NewPen(PS_SOLID, LS, RGB(0, 0, 255));
                 pDC->SelectObject(&NewPen);

                 pDC->Rectangle(x1, y1, x2, y2);
                }
                else
                {
                 // Set line size for each symbol separately
                 CPen NewPen(PS_SOLID, LS, RGB(255, 0, 0));
                 pDC->SelectObject(&NewPen);

                 pDC->Ellipse(x1, y1, x2, y2);
                }

                // Set font size for each text item separately
                SetUpFont(pDC,  FS);
                pDC->TextOut(x3,  y3,  pDoc->ShapeText[i]);
            }
        }

void  CVisDrawView::OnLButtonDown(UINT  nFlags,  CPoint  point)
{
    CVisDrawDoc* pDoc = GetDocument();

    if (pDoc->ShapeIndex >= 100)
        return;

    pDoc->ShapePos[pDoc->ShapeIndex]  =  point;
    pDoc->ShapeSquare[pDoc->ShapeIndex] = 1;   // Draw square

    //Save line and font sizes for this symbol
    pDoc->ShapeLine[pDoc->ShapeIndex]  =  LineSize;
    pDoc->ShapeFont[pDoc->ShapeIndex]  =  FontSize;

    pDoc->ShapeIndex++;
    pDoc->SetModifiedFlag();
    Invalidate();
```

```
        CView::OnLButtonDown(nFlags,    point);
    }

    void  CVisDrawView::OnRButtonDown(UINT  nFlags,  CPoint  point)
    {
        CVisDrawDoc* pDoc  =  GetDocument();

        if  (pDoc->ShapeIndex  >=  100)
            return;

        pDoc->ShapePos[pDoc->ShapeIndex]    =  point;
        pDoc->ShapeSquare[pDoc->ShapeIndex] = 0;   // Draw  circle

        //Save  line  and  font  sizes  for  this  symbol
        pDoc->ShapeLine[pDoc->ShapeIndex]  =  LineSize;
        pDoc->ShapeFont[pDoc->ShapeIndex]  =   FontSize;

        pDoc->ShapeIndex++;
        pDoc->SetModifiedFlag();
        Invalidate();

        CView::OnRButtonDown(nFlags,    point);
    }
```

The Serialize function in VisDrawDoc.cpp should be amended as follows:

```
    void  CVisDrawDoc::Serialize(CArchive&   ar)
    {
        if  (ar.IsStoring())
        {
            for  (UINT  i = 0;  i < ShapeIndex;  ++i)
            {
              ar  <<  ShapePos[i].x;
              ar  <<  ShapePos[i].y;
              ar  <<  ShapeSquare[i];
              ar  <<  ShapeText[i];
              ar  <<  ShapeLine[i];    // Save  line  and  font
              ar  <<  ShapeFont[i];
            }
            ar  <<  -1;
        }
        else
        {
            int x1 = 0;
            ShapeIndex = 0;
```

```
                      while (x1 != -1)
                      {
                        ar >> x1;

                        if (x1 != -1)
                        {
                               ShapePos[ShapeIndex].x  =  x1;

                               ar  >>  ShapePos[ShapeIndex].y;
                               ar  >>  ShapeSquare[ShapeIndex];
                               ar  >>  ShapeText[ShapeIndex];
                               ar >> ShapeLine[ShapeIndex];  //Load line and font
                               ar  >>  ShapeFont[ShapeIndex];

                               ShapeIndex++;
                        }
                      }
                  }
              }
```

2   Amend the OnDraw function as follows:

```
    void   CVisDrawView::OnDraw(CDC*  pDC)
    {
        CVisDrawDoc* pDoc = GetDocument();
        ASSERT_VALID(pDoc);

        pDC->SetMapMode(MM_LOENGLISH);   // Change  mapping  mode

        int x1, y1, x2, y2, x3, y3;  // Change to signed integers
        UINT LS, FS;

        UINT MaxIndex  =  pDoc->ShapeIndex;
        for (UINT i = 0; i < MaxIndex; ++i)
        {
            x1  =  pDoc->ShapePos[i].x;
            y1  =  pDoc->ShapePos[i].y;

            x2 = x1 + 10;
            y2 = y1 + 10;

            x3 = x2 + 3;
            y3 = y1 + 3;
```

```
          LS = pDoc->ShapeLine[i];
          FS = pDoc->ShapeFont[i];

          if (pDoc->ShapeSquare[i] == 1)
          {
           CPen NewPen(PS_SOLID, LS, RGB(0, 0, 255));
           pDC->SelectObject(&NewPen);

           pDC->Rectangle(x1, -y1, x2, -y2);  // Change y direction
          }
          else
          {
           CPen NewPen(PS_SOLID, LS, RGB(255, 0, 0));
           pDC->SelectObject(&NewPen);

           pDC->Ellipse(x1, -y1, x2, -y2);  // Change y direction
          }

          SetUpFont(pDC,  FS);
          pDC->TextOut(x3, -y3, pDoc->ShapeText[i]);  // Change y direction
      }
   }
```

3   Edit the AfxCore.rtf file, following the conventions specified in Chapter 8, and then rebuild the application.